Viet Cong
Repression and
Its Implications
for the Future

Viet Cong Repression and Its Implications for the Future

Stephen T. Hosmer

Heath Lexington Books
D.C. Heath and Company
Lexington, Massachusetts

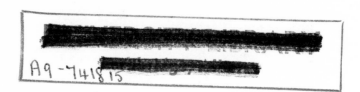

Printed in the United States of America

Library of Congress Number: 70-134013

Table of Contents

Preface

In this study, I have attempted to examine the Communists' use of repression as a major instrument of revolutionary warfare in South Vietnam, and to suggest how this practice, and South Vietnamese perceptions of it, may affect possible future developments in that country. For source material, I have drawn primarily on the voluminous files of enemy documents captured over the past several years, which strikingly illuminate both the Communist conduct of repression and the doctrine on which it rests.

While I alone assume responsibility for the contents of the book, and for the judgments it presents, I wish to acknowledge the valuable comments and suggestions of the several colleagues and friends who read and reviewed an early draft: Charles Cooper, Fred C. Iklé, Konrad Kellen, Guy Pauker, and Joseph J. Zasloff. I owe a particular debt to Sibylle O. Crane for her invaluable assistance in editing the manuscript, and to Rosalie Fonoroff and Shirley A. Lithgow for their able secretarial help. My thanks go also to Eve Savage, who prepared the Index, and to John C. Hogan, who arranged for the publication of this book.

This study is part of an ongoing program of research undertaken by The RAND Corporation for the Advanced Research Projects Agency, Office of the Secretary of Defense, into various military-political aspects of war termination in Vietnam. A slightly different version of this work was published in May 1970 as a RAND Corporation Report.

S.T.H.

Viet Cong Repression and Its Implications for the Future

1 Introduction

In the conduct of their fundamental strategy of revolutionary warfare, the Vietnamese Communists employ many and diverse instruments, both political and military. Designed to be mutually supporting, these are each focused on but one end: the seizure of political power in the South. The present study deals with one of the major instruments of this strategy, the systematic use of "repression." This is the generic term that the Vietnamese Communists themselves frequently employ for the broad range of measures by which they seek to eliminate, neutralize, punish, and reform their known enemies in the Government of South Vietnam and others whom they suspect of being hostile or unsympathetic to their movement. The spectrum of Viet Cong repression ranges from assassination, execution, and long-term imprisonment to such relatively mild disciplinary actions as compulsory indoctrination ("in-place reform"), forced confinement to village or hamlet ("home surveillance"), or several months in a thought-reform camp. These last, lesser measures often are used against persons whose only offense may be that they have some connection with the government, as well as against civilians who are deemed uncooperative or "unsympathetic" to the Revolution. It is, however, with the more severe actions and their victims—those GVN-connected persons who by occupation, deed, or ideological stance are regarded by the Communists as dangerous to their movement or responsible for "crimes" against the Revolution—that this study is primarily concerned.

One of the author's aims is to provide a comprehensive account of both the Communist practice of repression in the South and the doctrine supporting it, as they are revealed in the enemy's own documents. A second purpose is to examine some of the implications of these repressive activities and theories for the dénouement of the Vietnamese war. Clearly, the conduct of the South Vietnamese officials and military, be it on the battlefield or at the negotiating table, and the degree to which the people of Vietnam are prepared to continue resisting the Communists or inclined to accept compromise have been greatly influenced by the South Vietnamese' perception of the threat of repression in the event of a Communist victory. For many, the propensity toward accommodation with the other side depends largely on whether they believe that they are thereby ensuring their safety or hastening the day of a bloody reckoning.

Because the Communists' own testimony, as presented in captured documents, is most dramatically illustrative of their view and practice of repression, it constitutes the main body of the sources for this study. These documents, in their official English translations, have been allowed to speak for themselves, at some sacrifice of style and idiom.

A few words are in order here on the acquisition and processing of such materials. The Viet Cong, in the course of their day-to-day activities in the South, customarily commit to paper a great deal of information about their policies and operations. Not only does each of the numerous committees and specialized functional components, which exist at all echelons of the Communists' civilian and military structure, produce its own steady flow of directives, reports, and correspondence, but even individual cadres frequently maintain personal notes or diaries that chronicle the actions and missions of their units. Notebooks, diaries, private letters, and personal history statements normally are handwritten, as are some of the orders and directives of the smaller units. Official correspondence, orders, circulars, and directives at headquarters or Party committee levels, on the other hand, are usually typed. A smaller number of documents are printed; most of these are political, and are intended for political training.

The Communists employ several security classifications to protect their more sensitive documents. Viet Cong units use three different markings—Secret, Top Secret, and Absolute Secret—whereas the North Vietnamese Army forces use only two classifications—Secret and Top Secret.

Thanks to this copious output, Allied forces routinely capture a great many enemy documents; they find them in base areas that have fallen to Allied sweep operations, in bunkers protecting Communist bivouac sites, on the bodies of cadres killed in battle, and in the possession of prisoners of war. Standard procedure requires that, immediately upon capture, all documents be given an identification tag (known as "capture tag") showing the capturing unit's full organizational designation; the place of capture (with grid coordinates and map); the date and time of capture; and the circumstances of capture (whether found in a bunker, taken from a dead body, or acquired in any other way). This identification tag remains with the document throughout its subsequent exploitation.

All captured documents are forwarded to the Combined Document Exploitation Center (CDEC), a joint United States and South Vietnamese installation on the outskirts of Saigon. Materials found on prisoners of war are first sent to the interrogation centers along with the captives, and there serve as background for their questioning. Documents of immediate operational value are retained briefly by local headquarters for exploitation (the maximum period in most cases is fifteen days), before being forwarded to the CDEC. Upon arrival there, all documents are screened by analysts and classified according to their intelligence content. Those that seem to contain useful intelligence are given an identifying log number and are turned over to a corps of translators, whose English summaries of the significant information in each document are published daily in the form of MACV Bulletins. In addition, verbatim translations are prepared of all or portions of any documents that are thought to have particular intelligence value; they appear as Department of Defense Information Reports.[1]

The total amount of captured material that the CDEC handles is impressive; in 1967, for example, it ran to approximately 16,000 pages a day. Although only a small portion of it has enough intelligence value to merit exploitation, this still leaves the Center with a formidable output of summaries and translations—an average of 300 pages a day in mid-1969.[2] The aggregate of several years of this documentation is, of course, voluminous.

In the preparation of the present work, the author examined the output of the CDEC over the past several years for the information it might yield on the practice and doctrine of repression. The result of this search was the substantial body of documentation that constitutes the source material for this study: policy directives, resolutions, activity plans, attack orders, situation reports, minutes of Party meetings, circulars, indoctrination and training materials, correspondence, notebooks and diaries, rosters of persons executed or detained in thought-reform camps, blacklists of persons marked down for repression, and so forth.

Many of the documents have been produced by agencies of the Viet Cong Security Service, which has the primary responsibility for directing and implementing all repressive activities. Several comprehensive and authoritative policy directives originate with either the Central Office of South Vietnam (COSVN) or Military Region

Headquarters, and provide an excellent overview of the Communist stand on repression in general. These high-level documents are supplemented by numerous directives and activity plans issued by province and district headquarters and other subordinate echelons.

While these materials are very revealing of Communist policy with regard to repression, there is also substantial information on how local units attempt to carry out these policy guidelines, to be gathered mainly from the large number of activity and after-action reports that village, district, and province organizations must periodically submit to higher echelons.

Together, all these materials provide, by and large, a convincing and dependable picture of Communist doctrine and practice. Yet the reader should be aware of the inevitable shortcomings under which one labors in extrapolating from captured enemy documents. First, because all the sources used are translations, or summaries of translations, we cannot always be sure that the meaning and wording of the original have been rendered precisely. Second, not all the cover designations or codes with which the Viet Cong frequently mask the agency issuing a document have been broken, and it therefore is not always possible to identify the issuing unit with absolute certainty. Third, caution is indicated in the use of the Communists' claims of the numbers of GVN persons killed, figures that are difficult for the Viet Cong to verify and tend to be inflated. They have therefore been cited here only sparingly. Finally, the accuracy of Communist reporting is likely to be affected by a desire to put a good face on some very reprehensible actions, such as the killing of innocent relatives of GVN supporters—actions we know about from other sources but probably would not find listed by the Viet Cong under the proper rubric. (More likely, if reported at all, such murders would be included among "tyrants killed.")

Notwithstanding these handicaps in the evaluation of Communist sources on the practice of repression in South Vietnam, the available evidence does permit valid conclusions as to the scope and rationale of that instrument of Communist warfare. The main reason for this belief is the breadth of the documentation: the fact that the materials come from many units, which operate at various echelons of the military and political establishment in different geographic areas of South Vietnam.[3] The consistent picture of the general policy and mode of operations that emerges from this variety of separate sources is striking. Moreover, the evidence that we find in the captured documents seems entirely consonant with Allied reports on Communist repression in the South.

2

The Targets and Purposes of Repression

Throughout the present conflict in South Vietnam, the Communists, in their quest for political power, have systematically repressed large numbers of persons in certain categories (including civilian and military officials, security and intelligence personnel, and political party leaders) whom they consider, or suspect of being, particularly dangerous, or inimical to the success of their movement, and whom they label as "tyrants," "reactionaries," or "enemies of the people." The form as well as the severity of the repression will vary. Over the years, it has meant assassination, execution after capture, or extended confinement to thought-reform camps for tens of thousands of persons in the target categories. Many others, including countless villagers with only a marginal connection or allegiance to the Government of South Vietnam (GVN), have been subjected to the less severe "in-place reform" (compulsory indoctrination), "home surveillance" (forced confinement to village or hamlet), and short periods of confinement in detention camps. These and other forms of repression will be discussed in some detail in Chapter 4.

Repression has been a constant of Viet Cong policy in the South for over a decade. As early as 1957, the Saigon press was reporting an alarming incidence of assassinations and other repressive acts against "village chiefs, chairmen of liaison committees, simple guards, even former notables" in the countryside.[1] One observer, writing in 1958, contrasted this new pattern of activity with that of the Viet Minh during their struggle against the French:

While the wartime Viet Minh forces generally limited themselves to the intimidation of the local administrators (village chiefs, notables) into a state of positive neutrality, the new terrorists seek out the local police chiefs, security guards, village treasurers and youth leaders and kill them in as spectacular a manner as possible.

The objective of this rebel activity, said the writer, was the "gradual 'insulation' of the central authorities from direct contact with the grass roots."[2]

In recent years, as the ferocity of warfare in the South has mounted, so have the scale and intensity of repression, as is perhaps most clearly reflected in the rising number of assassinations and abductions. In 1958 and 1959, they were occurring at a rate of 400 to 600 a year. In 1966, over 5,500 assassinations and abductions were officially reported; in 1967, the number jumped to over 9,000; and the figure for 1968 was probably considerably more than twice that for 1967. (As will be noted in Chapter 4, these official figures probably understate significantly the actual number of assassinations and abductions during the years in question.) Far from being a mindless or random process, this repression has been a calculated and, for the most part, carefully managed operation designed to further specific political and military objectives of the Communists.

The Viet Cong Security Service

The primary instrument of repression in the South is the Viet Cong Security Service. Though seldom mentioned in the open literature, this important apparatus (which the Viet Cong often call *An Ninh*) has long been known to Allied intelligence. Estimated at between fifteen and twenty thousand members in 1966—the number today is put at over 25,000—this highly professional, ruthless organization operates in all areas of South Vietnam (Viet Cong-controlled, contested, and GVN-controlled) under close supervision from Hanoi. As an organic part of the Ministry of Public Security (MPS) in North Vietnam, it reports regularly to that Ministry, and each of its echelons above district level is at times subject to direct orders from the Ministry. Hanoi's control is further ensured by the fact that many key posts in the Security Service, from the Central Office of South Vietnam (COSVN) down to district and even village level, are held by MPS officials trained in the North. Their infiltration is known to have begun as early as 1960, and by 1967 was estimated to have reached a rate of five hundred or more men a year.

The Security Service is organized along pyramidal lines, with a 500-man headquarters located at COSVN, and subordinate echelons (Security Sections) at region, province, district, and village levels. Each echelon is immediately responsible, in the course of its normal activities, to the security hierarchy of the next higher echelon and to the Current Affairs Committee of the Party organization at its own level. Each Security Section is in turn divided into several Subsections with special functions. A typical Province Security Section, for example, might have a staff of over one hundred and be divided into four Subsections: an Administrative Subsection (B 1), which handles routine correspondence; a Political Protection Subsection (B 2), which runs internal security, Party security, and counterintelligence operations; an Espionage Subsection (B 3), which operates in government-controlled areas; and a Legal Affairs Subsection (B 4), which runs Viet Cong interrogation facilities and jails. The formal organization is in turn supported by a network of thousands of secret agents and informants in both rural and urban areas who have been recruited by local security cadres.

The Security Service performs a number of crucial missions in the South. One of its major responsibilities is to collect information on the various GVN security and intelligence agencies, and it devotes much time and effort to penetrating these organizations, as well as to injecting agents into South Vietnamese political parties and religious sects. Another major responsibility is the protection of "liberated" and Communist base areas against penetration by Allied intelligence. To this end, Security Service cadres track down and investigate anyone within their jurisdiction suspected of being a GVN agent, and keep close tabs on persons who may be sympathetic to the government. As part of this "internal security mission," security components at all echelons conduct intensive and frequent indoc- trination programs for both Viet Cong personnel and the general populace concerning the importance of maintaining security. A third major function of the security apparatus is to keep watch over all cadres and personnel serving in the Viet Cong infrastructure and ensure their political reliability. Security cadres maintain files on persons in local Viet Cong organizations whom they consider potentially unreliable, and are prepared to move swiftly and firmly against those who step out of line. All echelons of the Viet Cong bureaucracy, even senior officials, are subject to such surveillance. The chief of the Province Security Section, for example, if he sees fit, may bypass the hierarchy of the provincial bureaucracy and report on the activities of provincial officials—including the head of the Current Affairs Committee—directly to the Region Security Section.

Among the most important responsibilities of the security apparatus, however, are the direction and conduct of repression. As will be shown, it is the Security Service cadres who draw up the blacklists of the persons to be killed or incarcerated; who man the Armed Reconnaissance Teams which abduct and assassinate victims in GVN-controlled areas; who arrest, interrogate, and recommend punishment for persons that have been taken prisoner; who carry out the death sentences; and who maintain the detention facilities for prisoners of the Viet Cong. While other military and political units of the Viet Cong often take part in repressive activities and may even play a major role (as in hunting down persons in GVN-controlled areas), it is the Security Service which provides the leadership and over-all direction.

The Targets of Repression

One of the functions of the Viet Cong Security Service is to establish categories of persons who are to be the targets of repression. Following are the major target categories most frequently mentioned in Security Service directives and other captured enemy documents:[3]

- GVN officials and administrative personnel from the central government in Saigon down to the city-ward, hamlet, and interfamily-chief level.

- "Leaders and dangerous tyrants" in the Republic of Vietnam Armed Forces (RVNAF) and paramilitary forces, particularly officers and noncommissioned officers.

- Leaders and members of the GVN's intelligence and counter-intelligence agencies, including the Military Security Service (MSS) and Central Intelligence Organization (CIO), and all "spies," "informants," and "reconnaissance agents" in the service of these or other government agencies.

- Officials and personnel in the various GVN security organizations, including members of the National Police and Police Field Forces.

- "Chieu Hoi" ("Open Arms") and psychological warfare officials, Revolutionary Development cadres, Census Grievance Team members, and other GVN functionaries who operate at the village or hamlet levels.

- Officials and members of "reactionary" political organizations such as the Dai Viet and Viet Nam Quoc Dan Dang (VNQDD) parties, and persons who have been associated with the Can Lao.

— "Reactionaries" and persons "working under the name of religion" who "cause difficulties" for the Revolution.

— "Former" government administrative personnel, "reactionaries," and political party members "who still oppose" the Revolution.

— Viet Cong defectors and "the surrenderers and traitors who become enemy henchmen."

— "Other reactionary elements whose activities are harmful to the Revolution."

As one can readily see, these target groups cover a wide spectrum; in the words of one security directive, they include virtually all "elements who actively counter the Revolution and are working for the enemy system."[4]

In its planning of repression, the Security Service gives first priority to "ringleaders," "leading tyrants," and "the most stubborn elements" in the above target categories. Persons so characterized not only include key civilian officials and military officers but also lower-ranking personnel who are adjudged to have committed serious "crimes against the people" or who have obstructed the development of the Communist movement in a particular area. Thus, a local policeman might be labeled a "leading tyrant" in a particular village and put high on the list of persons to be assassinated. And an ARVN noncommissioned officer might be branded a "wicked tyrant," deserving of execution "on the spot" if captured.[5] Indeed, lower-level personnel, because of their larger numbers and easier accessiblity, make up the great bulk of the victims of repression.

Persons from any of the groups listed above may be targeted for the severest repression: assassination or execution after capture. To illustrate, a high-level directive issued by the Security Section of COSVN and captured in January 1969 ordered subordinate units to "destroy" the following:

Cruel tyrants working for the Puppet Government's machinery on every level (*first, they must kill* policemen, security and intelligence personnel, spies, informers, and anti-revolutionary leaders who are directly exercising oppressive control over the people and interfering with our activities in our areas of operation) . . . . Chieftains working in the enemy's police and security organizations, intelligence organizations, military security organizations, spies, informers, ralliers, members of pacification groups, persons who have surrendered to the enemy and committed crimes . . . and leaders of reactionary political organizations.[6]

A good example of the breadth of the spectrum of target categories in a given Viet Cong administrative area is provided by a Secret directive of May 18, 1969, attributed to an agency of the Can Duoc District Unit, Subregion 3. Village Security Sections and other subordinate agencies, it stated, were to consider the following categories of persons as "subject to disciplinary action" in the course of carrying out their mission of exterminating "wicked tyrants" and disrupting the "puppet" administrative and pacification organization:

Enemy public security personnel, intelligence personnel, military security personnel, RVNAF personnel, psywar personnel and pacification personnel, hamlet and village administrative personnel, civil self-defense members, informers, those in charge of appealing to our cadre to surrender, "Phoenix" spies, intelligence personnel working for both sides [double agents], and false defectors [from the GVN].[7]

The directive went on to specify quotas of persons to be eliminated by the different subordinate units. "Each armed reconnaissance cell" operating at the district level, for example, was to "kill at least one chief or assistant chief in each of the following: Public Security Service, District National Police Service, Open Arms Service, Information Service, Pacification Teams," as well as "a District Chief or an Assistant District Chief." In addition, "each [district] cell must exterminate three wicked tyrants living in district seats or wards, and warn thirty other enemy personnel that they will be punished if they do not conform by rallying to our cause." Village units were also assigned a quota, being told that each "must kill three enemy and send a warning to thirty other personnel." According to the directive, all these quotas were to be met during the month of June 1969.[8]

The Purposes of Repression

Disintegration of the GVN

The primary objective of repression is the disintegration of the GVN. Through the physical elimination, demoralization, and subversion of personnel at all levels of the government structure, the Viet Cong seeks progressively to erode and eventually to paralyze the GVN's capability to govern and secure those areas now under its control, as well as to blunt any attempts by the GVN to extend its control or influence into the contested or Communist-held areas. In the context of this fundamental objective, the logic underlying the target categories is readily apparent. Thus, the target lists embrace the leadership component of the GVN's administrative apparatus, both civil and military, from Saigon down to the hamlet. All the government's major instruments of control are included: the urban gendarmerie and rural Police Field Forces; the command echelons of the ARVN and the various paramilitary units responsible for local security in the rural areas; and the counterintelligence organizations charged with containing and eradicating Communist infiltration and subversion within the GVN structure. Also included are important anti-Communist political organizations and those religious leaders who "openly work against the Revolution." In short, the target lists incorporate key elements and supporters of the existing governmental structure who are the major barrier to a Communist assumption of power in the South.

Furthermore, the target categories encompass personnel from those GVN agencies which pose the greatest threat to the security and cohesion of the Viet Cong infrastructure and to the Communists' chances of maintaining control of "liberated" areas. They are the government's civilian and military intelligence organizations and the networks of agents and informants they manage; the Rural Development cadres, who, in the past, have constituted the cutting edge of the government's efforts to expand its control in the rural areas; the "Chieu Hoi" and psychological warfare cadres, who seek to undermine the Viet Cong's political and military infrastructure; and the Viet Cong defectors.

The Viet Cong view repression as crucial to the development and the protection of their revolutionary movement in both urban and rural areas. Thus, a Top Secret directive prepared by the Security Section of Region II in April 1967 stated that the "elimination of traitors and tyrants in cities is an indispensable mission to protect and serve the development of [our] movement." It continued:

While the movement in [the] cities evolves, the Party in the city has to step up the elimination of traitors and tyrants to press forward the disintegration of the enemy. The Party [must] also heighten revolutionary prestige and create favorable conditions for the strong advancement of the movement.

The elimination of traitors and tyrants must aim exactly at the objective. We have to wear down and destroy the most cruel and dangerous element of the enemy which is attacking and oppressing the movement. In this way, we can protect and serve the rapid development of the movement; heighten revolutionary prestige; increase confusion and doubt in the enemy's internal organization; create conditions to weaken their ranks; isolate stubborn tyrants; and, at the same time, diminish difficulties and complications for the coming counterrevolutionary repression.[9]

The directive went on to say that requirements "demand us to eliminate traitors and tyrants strongly, continuously and everywhere in cities." Specifically, it urged attacks on "the most dangerous counterrevolutionary concentrations" ("police," "military security agencies," "intelligence services," etc.) and the extermination of "the heads of political and reactionary organizations" who were "waiting for an opportunity" to "sabotage our movement." As the "present objectives for extermination" it listed:

The heads of puppet government at various levels (including ward [and] quarter administrative personnel and the wicked tyrants).
The leaders and dangerous elements in the oppressive machinery [SVN] counterespionage service [civilian] and counterintelligence service [military], and most active informers as well (overt and covert).
Leaders of reactionary elements who resist and attack the Revolution.
Leaders and the dangerous tyrants in various armed forces and paramilitary forces.[10]

A second Top Secret document, also issued by the Security Section of Region II, speaks of the elimination of "traitors and tyrants" as a "mission" aimed at "breaking the enemy's control" so as to "disintegrate [his] ranks" in the contested ("weak") areas:

Elimination of traitors and tyrants to disintegrate the enemy ranks is an important policy of the Party in weak areas. This mission aims at breaking the enemy's control and weakening their prestige and, in addition, raising our revolutionary prestige. It also aims at encouraging the people's movement to break the enemy ruling machine and gain the administration power in villages and hamlets for the people. *Through past activities we clearly understand that if we lack determination in breaking the enemy's grip, security agents, spies, pacification cadre . . . we cannot develop the people's revolutionary movement.*
In addition, we will meet difficulties in weak areas. *Therefore, if, when transferring from one area to another we do not strictly observe the policy of eliminating traitors, we will not achieve the mission.*
The requirement for eliminating traitors and tyrants is to annihilate the leaders, to demoralize others, and weaken the enemy's prestige to create encouragement among the masses. There are many ways to eliminate traitors [and] disrupt their ranks; such as kill them on the spot, abduct them, warn them, use thought reform and politically attack them to demoralize their ranks.

According to the degree of crime of each enemy we will have to use appropriate measures to punish him. [11]

According to Viet Cong doctrine, repression can promote the disintegration of the GVN in a variety of ways. In the above quotations, it is presented as an important vehicle for heightening "revolutionary prestige" and denigrating the stature of the GVN; the assassination, abduction, and public trial of government officials before "People's Courts" are ways of driving home the elementary message that Communist power is all-pervasive and that the government is too weak to ensure the security of its own officials, much less that of the general populace. At times, the Viet Cong will lay on assassinations simply to "show the flag" in a particular GVN-controlled area and thereby cast doubt on the government's capacity to provide local security. One example of this is provided by a captured activity plan prepared by an element of the Rung Sat Special Zone of Subregion 4 in November 1967, which directed that local units should annihilate at least one of the most important "tyrants" in each village in order to lower the prestige of the GVN's administration. [12]

But the primary object of repression is much more direct: It is the disruption and demoralization of the GVN's civilian and military bureaucracies, and is achieved, in the first instance, through the physical removal (by assassination, execution after capture, or incarceration) of substantial numbers of military and civilian officials, cadres, and intelligence personnel who perform important services for the GVN and who are not easily replaced. Another, broader purpose is to demoralize, neutralize, and paralyze those other government officials and cadres who may themselves escape repression for a time but who are fully aware of the fate of their less fortunate colleagues. Thus, by assassinating a selected number of hamlet officials in a given district, the Viet Cong hope to frighten other officials enough to force them to resign their positions; or to flee to the district town for protection (go into "exile"); or to become so security-conscious that they no longer carry out their prescribed duties effectively. The hamlet chief who refuses to sleep at home or who, afraid of an attack, is reluctant to move freely about his hamlet has, from the Communist point of view, been largely neutralized. The Viet Cong's accounts of their accomplishments in a given area, such as the following from a security agency in Gia Lai Province, are indicative of their aims:

After our attacks, puppet administrative personnel were demoralized. Some of them forsook the hamlet office to stay overnight at the District. Some succumbed to the Revolution and willingly accepted our various missions. Others . . . went to the District to tender their resignations. In various hamlets surrounding the town of An Khe, a great number of local [RVN] administrative personnel sent in their resignations, and the oppressive enemy control of the population was broken.[13]

As suggested by the above reference to administrative personnel in the An Khe area who "succumbed to the Revolution and willingly accepted our various missions," repression is intended to facilitate Communist proselytizing efforts among the GVN's civilian and military bureaucracies. Indeed, the Viet Cong, in their proselytizing of groups marked down for repression, frequently offer their targets an explicit choice: either to continue in their service of the GVN and risk certain punishment, or to join forces with the Revolution and earn clemency and perhaps even rewards from the Communists. This important facet of repression will be discussed in detail in Chapter 5.

*Control and Polarization of
the Populace*

Repression also serves as a means of establishing control in areas which the Viet Cong seek to "pacify," and as a major instrument in the consolidation of Communist control over already "liberated" areas. Captured documents often refer to this process as the "purifying" or "cleaning up" of an area (removing all "spies," "tyrants," and other GVN remnants), and "purging" the local population of "undesirable" elements (persons who are openly hostile to the Revolution or whose loyalties are suspect). Consider, for example, the following captured plans and directives, all issued in 1968:

An activity plan prepared by the Dai Loc District Party Committee of Quang Da Province on May 25, 1968, directed subordinate units to "liberate all hamlets and villages in the vicinity of the District seat, seize political power, establish a revolutionary government, *overthrow the enemy's village or hamlet administrations, eliminate hamlet spies and local administrative personnel, weed out undesirable elements among the people, and continuously pursue village and district local administrative personnel* to liberate the masses from their grip and pressure."[14]

Another activity plan, dated December 22, 1968, and attributed to the Binh Dinh Province Party Committee, described the Communist mission in newly "liberated" areas in these terms: "We should immediately get down to consolidating and maintaining the areas just brought under our control as part of our expansion program. Reorganize the people, *wipe out the last spies, and purge the people's ranks of elements held to be undesirable . . . .*"[15]

A third activity plan, issued by an unidentified village security section in the spring of 1968, directed armed security elements to annihilate local government personnel and to *clear the village of all suspects and reactionaries* so as to make it safe for troops from higher headquarters.[16]

A directive dated October 5, 1968, and attributed to the Political Section of Gia Lai Province stated that "it is necessary *to weed out undesirable elements* in areas where the troops will stop . . . and in areas which are prepared as stepping stones and troop-advance corridors of the army."[17]

Once the Viet Cong establish a strong presence in an area, they try to seal off the local population both physically and psychologically from any further contact with the GVN. They are particularly intent on denying the government all intelligence on Communist troop movements, bivouac sites, supply caches, and information relating to those who serve in their local military and political infrastructures. To inhibit intelligence penetration and collection in Communist-controlled or contested areas, the Viet Cong not only systematically identify and neutralize anyone suspected of being a GVN spy or informant, but they also impose and enforce very stringent regulations governing travel within the villages and hamlets and proscribing all unauthorized contact with GVN persons, including immediate relatives. Any villager found violating these local regulations is subject to disciplinary action and runs the risk of being thought a GVN spy, a most serious charge, as even faintly "suspected" agents often are incarcerated in thought-reform camps. Proven spies are harshly dealt with, and most are executed. Captured documents suggest that, in at least some localities, Communist security cadres have standing orders to "kill without mercy" any GVN intelligence or reconnaissance agents attempting to penetrate the area.[18] From time to time, captured "spies" are given public trials before "People's Courts" as a way of impressing the local population with the Revolution's firm attitude in the face of such activity.[19]

The local people also are subjected to constant and intensive indoctrination by security cadres regarding the importance of the "security maintenance mission," and are instructed to keep watch over the activities and contacts of their fellow villagers and to report immediately the presence of any strangers in their areas.[20] Part of this indoctrination is an attempt to imbue villagers with a deep hatred of all GVN intelligence personnel. One plan urged local cadres to "motivate the people to engage in security maintenance activities, arouse their hatred of enemy spies and intelligence personnel, and make them uncover the latter."[21] And a letter to a local Security Section in the Saigon area said that the main purpose of this mission was "to unmask the enemy's cunning schemes to the people in order to increase their deep hatred towards the enemy, especially the security agents, policemen, intelligence agents, spies and informants."[22]

The fomenting of hatred and vindictiveness is by no means limited to GVN intelligence personnel; indeed, all repressive activity is cloaked in a highly emotional propaganda designed to arouse the people to a deep hatred of, and a desire for revenge against, the military and civilian officials serving the government. According to captured documents, Communist cadres are called on to "deepen the people's hatred" toward the GVN, to "incite" their "wrath," to "arouse" their "hate against the Thieu-Ky puppet government," and to "heighten their concept of revenge."[23] For example, in guidelines for a propaganda campaign in Ben Tre Province for the period October 1968 to March 1969, the Viet Cong directed cadres to "make the people feel a profound hatred of [the] enemy's savage crimes and incite them to avenge their compatriots and kinfolk by enthusiastically and actively taking part in combat activities to heroically annihilate the enemy and achieve great merits."[24] Another propaganda directive, covering the same period but issued by a Region headquarters, urged them to "intensify [the people's] deep hatred for the enemy, [and] strongly and continuously denounce the savage and brutal crimes committed by the Americans and their lackeys towards our people."[25]

Frequently, these hate campaigns focus on specific targets of repression, as evident from a security directive, captured in March 1968, which outlined the types of propaganda that should accompany the repression of "counterrevolutionary elements":

While motivating the people to deepen their resentment of the enemy, we must so propagandize them that they can see the enemy's deceitful, demagogic, pacification schemes, and that the hamlet and village [RVN] administrative personnel, pacification cadre, and "people's aspiration" cadre, etc. . . . are but traitors, henchmen of the US Imperialists. They entice the people with mellow words while trying to deceive and exploit them. The theme our daily propaganda must be based on is concrete on-the-spot examples of enemy crimes.[26]

In expounding the various crimes of government personnel, Viet

Cong propagandists dwell on the many "inhuman" and "barbaric atrocities" allegedly committed by the Americans and their "GVN henchmen," the wanton destruction of homes and property, and the "rape," "murder," and "torture" of innocent men and women. Government officials are characterized as "Vietnamese traitors" who "fatten their lives on our blood."[27]

That the Communists have continued to give high priority to their "deep hatred for the enemy" movement is illustrated by this passage in a Secret directive concerning security activities, issued by an agency of the Can Duoc District Unit, Subregion 3, on May 18, 1969:

We must motivate the entire army and people to join the "deep hatred for the enemy" movement waged by us and be determined to sweep the enemy. We must seek all means to destroy people who surrender, traitors and pacification personnel.[28]

Such hate campaigns apparently have several objectives. One is to justify the most severe measures (assassinations and executions) taken against some government servants; indeed, the killing of "tyrants" is made to appear as a heroic act deserving special recognition and award.[29] The other is to warn any member of the general populace who might be tempted to treat with or join the GVN.

The central purpose of this hate propaganda is to polarize the population, to divide it irrevocably from the GVN, and to mobilize it for service and sacrifice in support of the Revolution. The people are to learn to view the war in black and white terms, to accept no coexistence with the GVN, and to fight the enemy without compromise. They must acquire "a clear-cut antagonistic attitude" toward the government, such as that described as follows in a report of the Military Affairs Party Committee of Area 3:

Attitude of the population: The people did have a clear-cut antagonistic attitude toward the enemy. They only wished the Revolution could emerge victorious as quickly as possible. This attitude reflected itself in the fact that they gave us information about the enemy police and spies, guided us to destroy cruel elements, sheltered us in their houses or showed us good positions in which to station our troops, provided us with material supplies and fed us.[31]

The ultimate aim of hate campaigns is to raise popular animus to such a pitch that the people will themselves participate in the liquidation of "spies," "tyrants," and "reactionaries." This objective was pressed hard during the General Uprising and General Offensive phase, which began during Tet of 1968, when Viet Cong propagandists and other political cadres were repeatedly urged to "promote the people's determination and enthusiasm in killing and capturing the tyrants." [32] More will be said of this later.

The Viet Cong Concept of Crime

Throughout the present study, reference is made to the "crimes" that allegedly have been perpetrated by those marked down for repression. Thus, the Communists in their blacklists give high priority to "investigating" and detailing the crimes of each individual, persons captured by the Viet Cong frequently are required to make a "full confession of all crimes," and those who wish to escape repression often are asked to "gain merits" in the service of the Revolution so as to "make up for past crimes."

By the standards of the Viet Cong, virtually any act harmful to their movement is a crime. For example, it is a crime to relocate villagers and to "herd" them into strategic hamlets. (Indeed, villagers who comply with relocation orders are themselves guilty, for "the act of obeying the enemy to dismantle the houses of the population is a crime."[33]) It is also a crime to collect taxes for the GVN and to "rob and gather rice" in food-denial operations,[34] as it is to "force the people to undergo political and military training"; to compel them to "pull day or night guard" duty; or to interfere with their free movement by sealing up "entrances leading to the city wards and hamlets."[35] Government officials who "force" civilians to join self-defense organizations are "tyrants" and criminals who merit death.[36] Similarly, GVN officials who attempt to uncover Viet Cong agents and infiltration networks by ordering changes in the identification cards issued to citizens are considered criminals and legitimate targets for assassination.[37]

It is a crime, furthermore, to "kill," "capture" and "detain" members of the Revolution, to burn or destroy the people's houses, to appropriate their land, to kill their buffalo or oxen, to extract bribes from them, to "scold" or "revile" the people, and to "oppress" them in any manner.[38]

All forms of spying are considered serious crimes. This applies not only to those active agents and informants who are under the direct control of GVN intelligence personnel and who may receive payment for their services but also to any villagers who may report on Viet Cong movements and activities or disclose the identity or location of Viet Cong personnel to ARVN units entering their hamlets. A villager in Subregion 1, for example, was ordered arrested and sentenced because he was suspected of having disclosed the location of a tunnel in his village during an ARVN sweep operation. Indeed, in Viet Cong usage the label of "spy" is interpreted very broadly and often is applied to persons suspected only of consorting or "sympathizing" with the GVN, and even to villagers who do no more than maintain contact with near relatives serving with the government. Almost any type of activity may constitute spying in Viet Cong eyes. An activity report from Subregion 4 spoke of "45 monks" in a local pagoda as "spies trained by the Americans," and referred to "local women and children" who had been employed by the enemy "to do all kinds of social work in order to inquire [about] and discover our actions . . . ."[40]

Attempting to flee from a "liberated" to a GVN-controlled area and deserting from a Viet Cong unit also are considered crimes. However, it is the defectors whom the Viet Cong regard as committing the most "tremendous crime" in that they provide "information to the enemy," who takes "advantage of it to sabotage our agencies and kill our compatriots and dear comrades."[41] A Secret memorandum prepared by the political staff of the Phuoc Long Province Unit in May 1966 reflects the Viet Cong's profound contempt for all deserters, and the MACV summary of this document shows that the Communists expect the worst of them:

Being afraid of death, deserters or traitors usually prepare for themselves a guarantee to vouch for their sincerity and gain the enemy's confidence and good treatment. These guarantees could be either the stealing and consequent disclosure of our classified military information, the seizure of our weapons and the killing of our cadre . . . .

Once these deserters have joined the enemy, they completely change their behavior and mentality. They commit numerous crimes against our armed forces and against the people in exchange for an egotistic and petty life. Some become very dangerous and continue to resist us even after the success of the Revolution.[42]

All such "traitors" are prime targets for assassination or execution should they fall into Viet Cong hands again.[43]

The very service of the United States and its Vietnamese "lackey government" is a crime in Communist eyes.[44] Military officers and civilian officials are criminals by virtue of the positions they hold, and the more vigorously and effectively these persons carry out their official duties, the greater their crimes. Thus, the dynamic official who attempts to organize his village against Viet Cong penetrations and actively combats the local Communist infrastructure is considered much more of a tyrant than is the passive official with a "live and let live" attitude toward the Viet Cong apparatus in his village. The Viet Cong also have a tendency to equate guilt with rank and with ideological firmness. Thus, the higher the official's position (the "high-echelon traitor"), and the more adamant his stand against communism ("the most stubborn elements"), the greater are his crimes.

All government servants, high and low, who have hurt the revolutionary movement or committed other serious crimes are regarded as owing a "blood debt" to both the people and the Revolution. The phrase frequently crops up in captured documents. For example, urban security cadres are urged to "keep records of the wicked individuals and those who owe a debt of blood to us so that we may properly convict them when we have liberated the city";[45] local units are directed to attack "tyrants" and pacification personnel who owe a "blood debt to the people."[46] Activity reports on the assassination or execution of GVN persons also frequently use the term. A December 1968 activity report from Hai Lang District, Quang Tri Province, for example, reported the killing of a "district security agent and wicked tyrant who had a blood debt toward the people" of some nine different villages, and who was "an instigator for suppressing our movement" in a tenth village.[47] Another activity report, covering operations in Tay Ninh Province between February 25 and March 25, 1967, reported the elimination of "6 pacification cadres and 5 tyrants and spies who had accrued blood debts," among them a "spy" and a "Biet Kich [Special Forces] assistant platoon leader" who had incurred "many blood debts"; a resident of a "New Life" hamlet "who had embraced the open-arms policy [fled to the GVN] and acquired many blood debts"; and a "village finance committee member" in a second "New Life" hamlet who had "amassed many blood debts, taken bribes, and exacted ruthless taxes."[48] These examples should suffice to suggest the large role that revenge plays in the Viet Cong concept of justice.

Flexibility and Restraint in Repression

As is the case with nearly every aspect of Communist operations in Vietnam, the strategy and conduct of repression are dictated largely by political considerations. Repression, far from being a mindless or random bloodletting, is, according to Viet Cong doctrine, a carefully calculated and controlled process designed to support the immediate objectives in each phase of the revolutionary struggle and closely integrated with other political-military operations. The Viet Cong leadership, therefore, at least until the Tet Offensive of 1968, has placed heavy emphasis at all echelons on the need to be flexible in the use of repression and to keep it well enough under control to avoid actions which might prove politically unwise.

The need for "flexibility" was the subject of a security directive issued by the Current Affairs Section of COSVN in November 1966, which stated that the process and severity of repression

varies in tone according to each particular area and at each particular period of time. [At times our repression is brutal.] At other times we must show a certain degree of leniency. But, in any case, as far as our [real] enemy is concerned, we must continue repressing him . . . . In certain areas, it is necessary to place more emphasis on the repression side to enhance the revolutionary prestige of the people and to eliminate the wanton acts of the enemy. In other areas, we must show leniency. But in no case should we push things to the extreme or be completely one-sided.[49]

Flexibility also permits the Viet Cong at times to direct their repressive activities against a particular government initiative. One such instance was the response to the GVN's Accelerated Pacification Program, initiated in the fall of 1968, which local Communist cadres were ordered to counter by "stepping up" their attacks on pacification team members,[50] and by penetrating the areas selected for pacification and liquidating "tyrants," administrative personnel, "spies," and "informants."[51] Another example can be found in the Viet Cong's attempts to neutralize the GVN's "Phuong Hoang" (Phoenix) operation—a combined intelligence and security effort designed to root out the Viet Cong infrastructure through the elimination or capture of leading Communists. Local cadres were urged to take the "initiative" and to "capture and annihilate" GVN persons involved in the Phuong Hoang organization "at all cost."[52] As one directive put it,

Our intent should be to individually destroy his [the enemy's] important personnel, especially their commanders, or to seize [them] and then extract information on [the Phuong Hoang] organization and networks . . . promptly discover enemy secret networks in the liberated areas and areas under mixed control. Punish them severely to foil their sabotage schemes.[53]

Captured directives also reveal a strong sensitivity to the danger that uncontrolled repression may lessen popular support for the Viet Cong. They warn against "reckless seizure and killing" and "the irresponsible punishment of innocent persons" which might weaken popular support. As stated in the aforementioned Top Secret security directive from Region II, in April 1967,

If we do not strictly annihilate tyrants or, on the contrary, we kill innocent people, we will make the people have false thoughts of the Party's policy and we cannot dislocate the enemy's rank. In addition, those acts will create favorable conditions for the enemy in promoting dissension between the people and the Revolution and [will] let them insert more tyrants.[54]

Lower security echelons are continuously reminded to comply strictly with regulations in the investigation, arrest, and punishment of targets, and to take particular care in "determining the proper target" and "differentiating between enemy and friend." In the words of the 1966 COSVN directive,

If we fail to make this distinction between our enemy and our friends, we will create additional complications and adversely affect the execution of the Party's policy. Our mistakes will multiply and take on gigantic proportions, our repression will widen in scope, which will result in a loosening of our grip over our real enemy. Furthermore, the enemy will avail himself of this non-distinction to engage in clandestine activities, spread distorted news about us and cause us many difficulties.[55]

In line with this general policy of avoiding actions that might cost popular support, Viet Cong security officials attempt to maintain particularly tight control over the repression of religious leaders, ethnic minority leaders, and other persons whose standing among the people is high. A 1965 security document, for example, stated that the arrest of religious leaders—such as Roman Catholic bishops and priests, Protestant ministers, Buddhist venerables and monks, and Cao Daist leaders—of ethnic minority leaders, and of persons enjoying a certain prestige in society should be decided by the Current Affairs Committee of the Region Party Committee only upon the recommendation of province or district units.[56] Similarly, the 1967 security directive from Region II urged local cadres to "use care in dealing with those who commit crimes but have warm support and prestige among the people."[57]

This is not to say that such persons are not to be targets for repression. It means, however, that the Viet Cong see a need to be circumspect in dealing with these popular leaders, and selective in repressing them. The captured documents provide strong evidence, for example, that the Viet Cong consider many Catholic, Buddhist, Cao Dai, and Hoa Hao leaders "reactionary" or "antirevolutionary."[58] Moreover, local security organizations are required regularly to draw up "blacklists" of such "reactionary" religious leaders, and these persons occasionally are ordered killed or, more frequently, incarcerated in thought-reform camps.[59] In comparison with their handling of other target groups, however, the Viet Cong have manifested considerable restraint in the repression of religious personalities.[60]

Viet Cong regulations also forbid the wanton murder, torture, and humiliation of military prisoners. This policy is based in part on the very pragmatic consideration that it is much more difficult to induce surrenders if prisoners are mistreated. A report of July 1, 1967, relating to military proselytizing activities in Military Region (MR) V sums up the rationale for correct treatment of military prisoners:

It is an advantage for us, not for the enemy, if the prisoner is properly implemented. Unless we spare the lives of captives in this battle, we cannot expect the enemy to surrender in future battles. If they surrender, we can prevent many casualties, thus accelerating our final victory.[61]

According to a notebook believed to have been maintained by a cadre of the 81st Battalion, it is even permissible in some instances for local Communist units to release rank-and-file prisoners on the spot when battlefield conditions make it difficult to remove them to rear areas. The notebook also stresses, however, that, even in these situations, prisoners who are "tyrants" must be killed at any price.[62]

It may be said, then, that the Communists have tended to view repression as a flexible instrument, to be applied in accordance with the political requirements of a particular area at a particular time. They have also been sensitive to the political dangers inherent in the misuse of this instrument, particularly to the possible loss of popular support, and have therefore attempted to keep it under firm control. Maintaining control became more difficult, however, with the launching of the Tet Offensive.

The General Offensive and General Uprising

The Tet Offensive of 1968 marked a significant shift in Communist strategy in Vietnam, for it introduced an entirely new revolutionary stage: the General Offensive and General Uprising. This strategic shift was accompanied by an important change in the intensity and scope of repression. In contrast to the doctrine of previous years, when the emphasis was on a controlled and flexible use of repression, closely geared to the tactical requirements of a given area, it now was seen as a central instrument for bringing about the rapid collapse of the GVN in both urban and rural areas, and was applied throughout the country on a greatly intensified scale.

As conceived by Communist strategists, the General Offensive and General Uprising involved a series of coordinated attacks on GVN installations in cities, towns, and villages, which in time would so weaken and demoralize the government that it would cease to function and ultimately would disintegrate. The first phase of this offensive was launched on January 31, 1968, during the New Year celebrations, with simultaneous assaults on Saigon and on 36 of the country's 44 provincial capitals, 5 of its 6 autonomous cities, and 64 of its 242 district capitals.[63]

Repression played a major role in the offensive, because the elimination of GVN officials, military leaders, police and other security elements was considered essential to breaking the government's "oppressive control" and creating the conditions in which the "masses" could be encouraged to "rise up" and establish "a revolutionary government." As one directive put it, "without the annihilation of tyrants and spies, there would be no uprising."[64] Throughout the attacks, major emphasis was given to the systematic elimination of key groups within the GVN. Blanket directives called upon attacking units to "rapidly root out, kill or capture wicked tyrants, local administrative personnel and spies"[65] and cadres were told that "violence" should be intensified to the highest degree and all "tyrants" assassinated.[66] One attack order, issued by the Presidium of the Central Committee of the National Liberation Front and captured on February 3, called upon "all military forces of the Liberation Army and militant political forces" to "dash forward" and "overthrow all levels of the stooge government and drastically punish all high echelon traitors and all tyrants."[67]

Indeed, it was virtually open season on key GVN officials and cadres. A Top Secret directive dated February 11, 1968, and attributed to the Current Affairs Committee of Subregion 1 authorized subordinate personnel to kill the leading cadres of "reactionary" organizations immediately upon capture, these organizations to include, specifically, RVNAF and GVN administrative agencies; National Police, Military Security Service, and airfield security elements; intelligence and espionage agencies; and political parties such as the VNQDD and Dai Viet. Lower-ranking members of these organizations were not to be summarily executed.[68]

In the course of the offensive, a concerted effort was also made to induce the local populace to participate in the repressive process by assisting the Viet Cong in tracking down "tyrants" and eliminating GVN officials. A high-level training document from this period emphasized that "the substance of the present political struggle is not 'to stage demonstrations to present petitions' but *to make use of violence to overthrow the enemy government and to establish the people's revolutionary administration.*" It went on to say:

Therefore, the key problem is *making preparations and motivating the masses to seethingly arise (in coordination with the military offensive) to annihilate cruel tyrants and wicked administrative personnel and spies, to smash the puppet government and the enemy reactionary machinery*, to establish the revolutionary administration, and to quickly develop the people's revolutionary forces.

To perform this task well, it is necessary to work out uprising plans for each local area (particularly for the villages) in a very concrete and careful manner and make them thoroughly understood by all Party members and popular organizations and to ensure that offensive and uprising plans, for local areas, will include offensives, uprising and also enemy troop proselytizing activities. In these plans, *it is necessary to specify the specific mission of each Party cell, each organization cell and each Party member concerning the annihilation of cruel tyrants, ring leaders, spies and lackeys of the enemy in district seats, towns and cities as well as special mission agents*, to eradicate all forms of oppressive enemy control, to smash the puppet government system; to establish the people's revolutionary administration; to develop popular organizations, which should be viewed as a *decisive link* in the motivation and leadership of the masses to arise and seize and hold the power.[69]

An activity plan of February 5 outlined how the masses were to be motivated and organized to "annihilate" government persons, including pacification cadres and to track down the "remnants of the enemy troops":

We must continuously motivate the masses to track down and completely annihilate puppet government agents and installations in the rural area (including all of the pacification forces). Then, we must track down and completely annihilate key personnel of the administration at district and province levels and partially annihilate the central level (including the intelligence, espionage and security networks) to completely break the enemy's oppressive control [over the population]. We must destroy the entire reactionary political forces in towns, cities and district capitals and continue to liberate the remaining jails and prisons. We must also set up Liberation Committees in various wards, districts, provinces, and cities which have been occupied by our forces. We must quickly consolidate and expand the [revolutionary] government at its very foundation and formulate various policies.

We must quickly increase the number of efficient political agents among the masses on a broad and firm basis, and teach them how to master the situation in towns and cities. *We must quickly organize the masses to make them participate in all tasks concerning town and city administration such as: tracking down the remnants of the enemy troops; suppressing anti-revolutionary elements*; maintaining order and security; organizing civil anti-aircraft defense, administering public services necessary for the livelihood of the people and combat activities of our troops, etc. [sic] . . . .[70]

To precipitate local uprisings, Communist front organizations disseminated appeals to the masses to annihilate their GVN oppressors. One such appeal, issued by the Saigon-Gia Dinh United Liberation Youth Association, urged people and students in the Saigon area to courageously stand up and suppress tyrants; punish the police and security agents, informants, and "wicked persons"; and accuse the chiefs of city wards and interfamilies of cruelty.[71]

Despite such urgings and efforts to foment popular uprisings, the Communists' attempts to enlist the support of local populations in their offensive apparently met with very little success. Indeed, Communist postmortems of the Tet Offensive mentioned this failure to spark popular participation as one of the major shortcomings of the campaign.[72]

Throughout 1968 and well into 1969, as the Communists sought to continue the General Offensive, destroying the "Puppet Government at all levels" and liquidating "stubborn ringleaders and tyrants" remained high on the list of important missions.[73] Documents produced in the fall and winter of 1968 continued to emphasize that "revolutionary violence" would determine the success of the political struggle and that it was the most efficient means for advancing political movements in the cities and towns.[74] A directive of November 10, 1968, attributed to the Political Department of MR V Headquarters stated that the main mission of guerrilla and self-defense forces was to cooperate with district and city units in annihilating the GVN's structure in cities, towns, and surrounding areas; eliminating enemy administrative personnel, police, pacification cadres, and Popular Force cadres; and thus provoking civilian uprisings.[75] A Top Secret plan dated December 12, 1968, believed to have been issued by an agency of Binh Dinh Province, directed that all government administrative and intelligence personnel who attempted to oppose the political struggles and uprisings of the masses be killed at any price.[76]

In attacks on urban areas, some units were ordered to concentrate on senior GVN commanders and officials. For example, a June 1968 directive prepared by a unit of the Tri-Thien-Hue Military Region stated that

the selection of important and key targets has a great significance affecting our common victory. We should, according to each town and city, select . . . targets such as the Puppet troops and government's ringleaders: Province Chiefs, Civil Guard Provincial Group Commanders, Security Service Chiefs, Mayors, Army Corps Commanders, Division Commanders, etc. . . . with their (administrative) machinery.[77]

Other units were instructed to concentrate on the very lowest levels of the organizational structure and proceed on a street-by-street basis to systematically root out and eliminate "reactionary" elements. Thus, a Viet Cong plan captured in November 1968, which outlined forthcoming operations against the capital of Ben Tre Province, directed local armed reconnaissance units to "update" their blacklists of lower-level GVN personnel in "each area inside and outside the city" and then proceed to eliminate these persons. Specifically,

There must be a plan to kill from three to five [reactionary elements] and put out of action from five to ten others on each street, in each bloc of houses. Loosen the enemy's oppressive control machinery, destroy 70% of the inter-family chiefs and 100% of the administrative personnel in the area. Tyrants are to be cut down and warning notices sent to (undesirable) elements forcing them to resign their posts.[78]

The setting of quotas on the number of government persons to be eliminated by individual units was characteristic of the General Offensive period. A sapper unit in the Quang Da Special Zone, for example, was instructed to kill a total of 100 tyrants;[79] a district force in Thua Thien Province was ordered to "completely des-troy . . . 200 tyrants."[80] A captured letter dated July 1968 concerning the conduct of security activities in Ben Tre Province called upon components of the Security Service to try to destroy 50 per cent of the GVN's administrative, police, and public security agencies at provincial, city, and district levels during a forthcoming phase of the offensive. Key cadres from the police, security, military intelligence, and psychological warfare agencies, along with village and hamlet administrative council members, were pinpointed as the main targets for liquidation.[81]

Quotas were imposed particularly in villages and hamlets, where local security elements frequently were asked to eliminate a specific number of "tyrants" or other GVN-connected persons. An activity plan adopted during a guerrilla warfare congress held by the Tuy An District Unit of Phu Yen Province in November 1968 listed a half-dozen hamlets, each harboring from one to seven "cruel tyrants" who were to be killed.[82] Another plan, from the Go Mon District Unit of Subregion 1, urged local units to kill from two to three "tyrants" in each village.[83] A third plan, prepared in December 1967 by the Command Committee of the Chau Duc District Unit of Ba Bien Province in anticipation of the Tet Offensive, assigned these targets:

Break the enemy grip. Destroy the three village administrative personnel in Phu My, Phuoc Thai [and] Phuoc Hoa Villages along Highway No. 5. Kill the 10 hamlet administrative personnel, 3 people's council [members] and other [personnel of] reactionary political organizations.[84]

In some instances, the number of targets for a single village was very high. Correspondence attributed to an agency in Binh Dinh Province and dated early August 1968 revealed that subordinate village organizations were being asked to assassinate twenty-five GVN officials, including pacification cadres, in each village.[85] Similarly high quotas were assigned in other areas.[86]

Inevitably, the initiation of the General Offensive and General Uprising greatly intensified Communist repressive activities throughout South Vietnam; in 1968, the number of assassinations and abductions alone was probably more than twice that of the previous year. Even so, the Viet Cong did not achieve anything like the results they had hoped for. The people did not "rise up" and participate in the repression, and most of the target quotas fell far short of fulfillment, mainly because Republic of Vietnam Armed Forces (RVNAF) and United States troops prevented any sustained Communist control of the urban areas, while many of the targets in the rural areas either went into hiding or fled to the safety of the towns and cities. The major exception to this was Hue, where Communist forces held a large part of the imperial citadel for some twenty-five days in February and thus had sufficient time and control (two conditions not afforded them in other urban areas) to be able methodically to track down local officials and other target groups. According to Communist estimates, which tend to be supported by actual body counts, about three thousand people were killed during the occupation of Hue.

3 The Blacklists

For some years, the Viet Cong have assiduously compiled blacklists of large numbers of persons in both urban and rural areas of South Vietnam whom they choose to classify as "tyrants," "reactionaries," "counterrevolutionaries," spies, or, simply, opponents of their movement.

The categories of individuals on these blacklists include government officials, military officers, police and other security personnel, intelligence agents and informants, pacification and Chieu Hoi cadres, Viet Cong defectors, members of political parties, and various religious leaders. By no means restricted to key officials, the blacklists encompass a spectrum ranging from senior leaders in Saigon to low-level administrators and informants in the hamlets. These are the persons whom the Viet Cong have marked down for repression.

There is strong reason to believe that the number of persons already listed in Viet Cong dossiers is considerable. This assumption is supported by the high priority that the Communists have consistently assigned to the compilation of such lists at all levels of their security organization, from region down to village and hamlet, and also by the fact that the categories of persons who are candidates for blacklisting are themselves very large.

The Types of Targets Listed

Some idea of the size and composition of the groups targeted for "investigation" can be garnered from two authoritative security directives, both marked "Top Secret," that were circulated by Region II to lower echelons in May 1967. The first, concerning the "intensification of the struggle against spies and reactionaries" in the cities, listed the following as "objects to be investigated":

Spies of the U.S. and Puppet Governments.
Oppressive counterespionage and security organizations . . . including various police agencies, prisons, detention camps, military security service, and military police.

Reactionaries including various reactionary parties, reactionaries among religious and ethnic minorities, other political and reactionary organizations, and the heads of people's legally established organizations in the cities. Pay special attention to the Dai Viet and Viet Nam Quoc Dan Dang parties as well as reactionary Buddhist and Catholic functions.
The personnel of [the] Puppet Government . . . .
Organizations of the enemy's armed forces.[1]

The second directive focused on the "mission of eliminating traitors and tyrants" in critical rural areas, and listed among targets to be investigated the GVN "administrative machinery, regional force, police, pacification cadres, civilian spies, Chieu Hoi cadres, psywar cadres, Biet Kich, soldiers, . . . reactionary associations, . . . secret agents, spies, and informers operating separately in villages and hamlets." Attention was to be paid to "tyrants, non-aligned persons, negative persons, and the crime each enemy has committed against the people to hamper our movement."[2]

In addition to instructing subordinate elements to uncover such traditional intelligence as the "organizations," "activities," and "plots" of enemy agencies in the cities and the "political, military, economic, and pacification schemes" in the countryside, both directives stressed the importance of compiling blacklists on each target group. In the cities, subordinate units were to "make a list of names and maintain the documents on counterrevolutionary individuals"; in rural areas, village Security Sections were ordered to "list counterrevolutionary elements and study each man to propose appropriate measures to be taken by the Chapter Committee." Both documents made it clear that the systematic production of blacklists was an essential part of the Viet Cong campaign of repression. The urban directive called thorough investigation "an indispensable requirement for the immediate and long-range struggle against spies and reactionaries"; in the words of the rural directive, "the first condition of eliminating traitors and tyrants is to properly assess the enemy situation."[3]

Similar guidelines concerning the importance of identifying targets for repression appear in other documents captured in the past few years. One of these, apparently written in 1964 and devoted to the mission of liquidating the reactionaries, said that "we must know well the background of individuals working for the oppressive agencies and intelligence or reactionary organizations (their names, residence, friends, and acquaintances) . . . . "[4] A province directive issued in August 1966 disclosed that the Viet Cong did not limit its blacklists to persons *currently* active as spies or counter-revolutionaries, but also desired those to be listed who had participated in such proscribed activities. Its instructions to local security elements were:

Know the activities of the counterrevolutionaries; all kinds of spies, reactionaries and saboteurs *(both past and present)* within the township; closely watch the spies and reactionaries in the township (make careful note of them in a notebook, and if you go away on long TDY or are reassigned, turn these individuals over to another comrade for surveillance); investigate all types of suspect individuals . . . . "[5]

A year later, another provincial directive asked subordinate echelons to "register all personnel working in the enemy's administrative machinery, from province to hamlet levels, and [thereby] create conditions for their elimination later."[6] Still another security directive, apparently issued by the 5th North Vietnamese Army (NVA) Division in August 1967, provided guidance on the liberation of the lowlands and rural areas in Military Region V and instructed subordinate elements to do careful reconnaissance and prepare complete dossiers on local administrative personnel and government spies.[7]

Among other captured directives on the investigation of target groups are several relating to village organizations, which will be discussed below.

The Uses of the Blacklists

The role of the blacklists in the Communist scheme of operations is clear. In the first place, they provide a roster of targets from which individuals can be selected for repression at any time. Once a list is compiled, a copy is usually passed on to either the local Party Committee or to higher security echelons for a decision as to which persons on it are to suffer immediate repression and what form the repression will take in each case, the main choices being abduction, assassination, or warning in GVN-controlled areas, and indoctrination, confinement, or execution in the "liberated" areas. Thus, a directive issued by a district in Ba Bien Province in November 1967 instructed subordinate villages to conduct a thorough investigation of all local RVN administrative personnel, so that appropriate action (namely, assassination, abduction, or warning) might be taken against them.[8] Another example of this use of the blacklist is provided by a letter dated August 1968 and attributed to a Communist agency in Binh Dinh Province, which instructed village elements to submit rosters of local GVN officials who were to be annihilated or warned, and to include biographic data and details of their "crimes." It went on to request that these village elements attempt to assassinate some twenty-five GVN officials, including pacification cadres, in each village.[9]

A long-range purpose of the lists is to provide a master roster of enemy personnel, so that, once the Viet Cong gain control of an area, they can systematically seek out and deal with individual targets. (There were numerous reports of this use of blacklists during the Tet Offensive in Hue and other cities.) The aforementioned Top Secret directive from Region II concerning the repression of reactionaries in urban areas was explicit on this aim:

Have the enemy situation in hand to serve the common activities of eliminating traitors in cities; carefully keep the names and records of counterrevolutionary individuals; classify these elements and suggest an examination to be able to take the initiative to eliminate them in every situation and prepare the coming counterrevolution repression.[10]

The Thua Thien Province Security Section told subordinate agencies in August 1965 to develop underground security personnel in areas temporarily controlled by the enemy, to investigate the state of enemy activity, and to classify targets according to whether they were to be sentenced to death, arrested, reformed, or indoctrinated on the spot, in order to prevent a confused situation when the area was "liberated."[11] And a provincial plan for 1966 called upon city security elements to "thoroughly investigate the areas of activity of the enemy agents, agencies, and puppet authorities of the Province" and to "keep records of the wicked individuals and those who owe a blood debt to us so that we may properly convict them when we have liberated the city."[12]

One instance of the intention to use the blacklist in this manner was provided by a plan dated October 22, 1968, which set forth instructions for organizing a "mass uprising" in a hamlet in Hoa Vang District, Quang Da Special Zone. Part of the scheme was to encourage local inhabitants to participate in the annihilation of government administrative and intelligence personnel in the hamlet, and the plan listed the names of twenty individuals who were to be killed.[13]

Blacklists are also used as a means of keeping track of pro-government persons who move from one area to another. When an individual who has been marked for repression is transferred from one hamlet to another, a notation is made in the local blacklist as to the place of his reassignment. Similarly, when officials flee an area because of Viet Cong operations, an attempt is made to determine and note their new locations. A letter dated December 20, 1967, to district elements in Quang Da Province requested that separate reports be prepared on ten categories of GVN personnel who had fled to Da Nang, Hoi An, Vinh Dien, or Saigon after the National Liberation Front had taken over their home areas. Among the categories specified were chiefs of interfamilies, members of local administrative councils, members of Civilian Irregular Defense Groups (CIDG), Regional Force personnel, and policemen.[14]

How the Lists Are Prepared

Primary responsibility for compiling the blacklists resides with various elements of the Viet Cong security apparatus at the region, province, town, district, and village levels. Above village level, there usually is an organizational division of labor between subsections responsible for conducting investigations in GVN-controlled areas and those that focus on Viet Cong-controlled and contested areas. In the province, for example, an element of the Espionage Subsection (B 3) of the security apparatus is in charge of running investigations in government-controlled regions and drawing up blacklists on various target groups in these areas, while responsibility for investigating reactionaries, spies, informants, or anyone suspected of sympathizing with the GVN in Viet Cong-controlled territory rests with the internal investigation element of the Political Protection Subsection (B 2). A similar division exists at the district level, where again the Espionage Subsection draws up blacklists for the district capitals and other government-controlled areas, while the mobile reconnaissance element of the Internal Security Subsection collects data and maintains files on suspected and "reactionary" individuals in enemy-controlled and disputed areas. In the villages, where security sections are much smaller, each organization keeps lists of those in its jurisdiction suspected of being on the side of the GVN. (It should be noted that village Security Sections operate in liberated, contested, and GVN-controlled areas.)

In their investigations, the Security Sections and Subsections employ a wide range of accepted intelligence and counterintelligence techniques, such as using secret agents, keeping government installations under surveillance, enlisting cooperative civilians as informants, relying on information gained from the interrogation of defectors or prisoners, and exploiting documents captured or stolen from the GVN.[15] The major source of information appears to be the extensive network of secret agents and local informants which the Viet Cong security apparatus has developed over the years in both urban and rural areas. Here are but a few examples: An entry of May 1968 in a notebook maintained by the leader of an intelligence cell in Hue City showed that the writer was planning to use a pedicab driver to obtain the addresses and locations of persons at the Headquarters of the 1st RVNAF Infantry Division and in GVN administrative offices in Hue City.[16] A Viet Cong informer in Da Nang City revealed in a captured letter that he had prepared rosters of GVN personnel in his area.[17] And an intercepted conversation between two Viet Cong agents made it clear that one of them had found out the names and missions of various agents employed by an intelligence agency through his acquaintance with a telephone operator and with the Chief of the Administrative Section of that agency. Having gathered the information on these people, the agent was overheard as saying that he would "find their homes" and help his colleague "get rid of them."[18] Another common way of collecting information is through interrogation. The Security Service stresses that, wherever possible, all knowledgeable personnel must be interrogated prior to punishment or execution. A Top Secret report dated February 20, 1968, and prepared by the Political Staff of Subregion 1, disclosed that a former Viet Cong who had defected to the government and then had again fallen into Communist hands had revealed, under interrogation, the names of twenty-nine other Viet Cong defectors from his Chieu Hoi center who were currently working for the GVN or for a U.S. intelligence agency in his area.[19]

The amount of information compiled on each individual appears to differ from one blacklist to another. In most cases, it probably depends on the efficiency of the local security element responsible for producing the lists and on the extent to which it has been able to develop reliable agent nets and other sources of information within various target groups. Ideally, the Security Service would like to have considerable detail on each person, as suggested by a directive of the Security Section of MR I, which urged subordinate units investigating "typical targets" to note clearly "whenever feasible" the "name in full, age, social class, place of birth, residence, relatives, position, period of time working for the RVN Government, special identifying marks, and crimes of each individual . . . . "[20] Prior to the launching of operations in particular areas, security subsections are sometimes required to attach maps to their blacklists showing the residence of each target. For example, a Secret directive for district security cadres prepared by a provincial security element of Subregion 1 specified that investigations of "targets" residing in towns were to include sketches of every town showing the location of the home and secret underground shelter of each target, as well as information on his place of work and routine activities.[21]

A number of captured documents contain such maps.[22] But many lists are much less complete, often giving only the names, positions, and addresses of the individuals involved. One item of information which seems to be stressed in all investigations is a listing of the individual's crimes, which is important as a basis for determining the appropriate punishment once the target is accessible to the Viet Cong. As one directive put it,

To prepare for [the] annihilation of tyrants, we must carefully investigate and thoroughly understand each individual's crimes in compliance with our requirements in order to report to Chapter [Party] Committee which will report to the District [Party] Committee for consideration and approval.[23]

Examples of Urban and Rural Blacklists

A number of blacklists have been captured by U.S and Allied units in Vietnam, but very few, if any, of them are master rosters including all targets in a major geographic area. Rather, the great majority are "operational lists," either of persons in a limited area (such as a precinct in Saigon or a hamlet targeted for Viet Cong operations) or of individuals connected with a particular GVN agency or local "reactionary" organization (such as a political party). These are some of the examples:

— One list containing the names, positions, and addresses of some 94 GVN military officers, civilian officials, and political party members in Hue. Among them are several senior ARVN officers ranking from Lieutenant Colonel to General; a number of key provincial and district officials; important police officials and members of the Provincial Security Service; various intelligence officials and agents; Rural Development and Psychological Warfare officials; and prominent members of the Dai Viet and VNQDD parties in Hue. Also listed are a number of restaurants, coffee houses, and hotels known to be frequented by high-ranking "puppet" personnel.[24] This apparently was only one of several blacklists used in the Hue area.[25]

— Two notebooks listing the names, positions, and places of residence of some 180 "wicked personnel"—officials or members of various political parties in two districts of Quang Tri Province. Of those listed, 97 are members of the Can Lao, 50 belong to the VNQDD, and 34 to the Dai Viet Party. One notebook also lists eleven other persons (including several police agents and an information cadre) as having been marked for execution by the Executive Committee of the local District Party Committee.[26]

— Two rosters prepared by an unidentified agency of Subregion 2, the first listing the names and positions of 110 members of the RVN Central Intelligence Organization and the second giving the names, positions, and addresses of 35 members of the Saigon police described as "tyrants." The latter document also recommends that further investigations be undertaken to obtain the addresses of an additional 35 members of the Saigon police who are thought to be tyrants.[27]

— A blacklist giving the names and positions of 13 senior police officials in Saigon, including the chiefs of the Port Police, Traffic Control Police, and various public security branch and police stations. All these officials are classified as "tyrants," and the list contains the notation that additional investigation will be needed to establish the home address of each.[28]

— A roster dated April 30, 1968, listing names and addresses of four security agents and one block chief in the Saigon area, and indicating that two of the security agents are armed with pistols.[29]

— A notebook belonging to a cadre of a District Security

Subsection which contains several rosters of RVN administrative personnel marked for execution.[30]

Other captured blacklists include rosters of Vietnamese employees of U.S. agencies in Hue,[31] of various district intelligence agents and informants,[32] and of students attending a GVN intelligence course in Cholon,[33] as well as lists of deserters and defectors from Viet Cong units. One such roster, prepared by an unidentified security agency, listed the names, ages, former positions, and dates of defection of 170 Viet Cong cadres and men (including 76 guerrillas) who had rallied to the GVN from seven different hamlets and villages during 1966 and 1967. The roster also indicated that a number of these defectors had been working for U.S. agencies.[34]

A large part of the Viet Cong's blacklisting concerns personnel in the hamlets and villages, and village Security Sections are under constant pressure to produce dossiers on a wide variety of targets at this level. A letter on the "Mission, Policy and Security Tasks for the Last Six Months of 1967" in an unidentified province contains this revealing passage:

We must know how many cruel elements there are among the village and hamlet administrative personnel, their homes, their offices, and places where they usually come to play.

See how many petty tyrants there are among the pacification teams, who the commanders are; what elements these pacification teams consist of and how many police field forces, "people's aspiration," and Civil Health Service elements there are.

See how many intelligence agents there are in the villages and hamlets, to include both the overt and covert types, and how many people they suspect.

See how many religious factions there are which are serving the enemy or may cause damage to our activities.

See what types of soldiers the enemy armed forces have, their weapons, names of their commanders . . . . [35]

Similar targets were listed in a Secret directive of October 1967 from a district Security Section, which instructed village units to obtain the names of "wicked" GVN administrative personnel such as hamlet and village officials, pacification and civic action cadres, covert security agents, policemen, soldiers, and Chieu Hoi, psychological warfare, and civil health cadres, and to submit them to village Party chapters for determination as to the appropriate prosecution and punishment. The culprits' dossiers were also to be forwarded to the Current Affairs Committee of the District Party Committee for its consideration.[36]

The demand for blacklists at the village level intensified with the approach of the General Offensive and General Uprising, which was to begin during Tet of 1968. The notebook of a village security cadre, in an entry dated January 23, 1968, revealed that the number of covert agents in his area would have to be increased to support the intensified terrorist activities that were being planned against local GVN officials. It made mention of a "Plan T," which called for a complete investigation of local GVN administrators and RVN military personnel in conjunction with this effort.[37]

In some instances, local security elements actually establish quotas for the number of persons to be blacklisted in a given period. A district activity plan for the 1967/1968 winter-spring offensive, for example, called upon subordinate Security Sections to "record the biographic data of 80 per cent of the village and district administrative personnel, public security agents, intelligence agents, reconnaissance agents, and spies in order to serve the revolutionary policy."[38]

Following are a few examples of the village-level lists captured in recent years:

— A notebook with entries dated between December 1967 and April 1968, maintained by a village cadre in Phuoc Long Province, listing the names and activities of GVN personnel who were assigned to his village, including persons connected with various GVN security agencies, the National Police, village and hamlet administrative organizations, and reconnaissance and civic action teams.[39]

— A notebook maintained by a district security cadre in Subregion 1, with entries dated from March to May 1968, listing the names, addresses, and activities of hamlet and village authorities, members of the hamlet civil defense organization, local GVN informants and military intelligence agents, and Political Action Team members operating in various hamlets. The notebook also recorded the names of nine youths from one hamlet who were said to be attending a GVN training course for pacification cadres in Vung Tau.[40]

— A report dated August 18, 1967, containing the name of a Viet Cong defector and 27 GVN officials working for various agencies (e.g., the National Farmers Association, the National Credit and Agricultural Agency, and the Chieu Hoi Ministry) in two villages of Gia Dinh Province.[41]

— A report dated November 20, 1966, prepared by a village Security Section of an unidentified province, listing the names of village and hamlet administrative personnel, police agents, persons who had defected to the GVN, former GVN administrative personnel, soldiers from the village now serving with the GVN, "suspected persons," and "persons who are against Revolution." Included in the list of suspects were persons who had frequent contact with GVN personnel or who were "prejudiced" against Viet Cong cadres. Among those characterized as being against the Revolution were several whose close relatives had been killed or captured by the Viet Cong for spying.[42]

Such blacklists, however, by no means convey the full range of investigatory activity, for the enemy uses many other forms of classification for the population of villages and hamlets. Sometimes, for example, villagers are divided into three or more categories (marked A, B, C, etc.) according to their attitude or behavior toward the Revolution. One such classification effort was reported by the Security Section of Ca Mau Province as having been based on a census of March 1965, in which some 5,396 "bad elements," including 726 women, had been identified in Viet Cong-controlled and "disputed" areas in the province and had been broken down as follows: *Category A* ("bad elements" who refused to cooperate with the Viet Cong even after attending thought-reform courses)—1,496 persons, including 196 women; *Category B* ("former enemy collaborators" who had "not changed much" after attending the thought-reform courses and who tended to adopt a "wait-and-see philosophy")—2,055 persons, including 287 women; and *Category C* ("bad elements" who were ready to cooperate with the Viet Cong after attending thought-reform courses)—1,845 persons, including 243 women.[43]

Persons appearing on such lists are normally kept under surveillance by local security cadres and, depending on their performance and attitudes, may be moved to other lists. Those who remain on the "A" list are prime candidates for repression. This investigation and classification appears to be a large-scale effort. The Security Section of Military Region III, for example, reports that its subordinate echelons recorded the names of 8,086 suspected persons in the month of February 1966 alone.[44] Another report, captured in January 1969 and attributed to the Security Section of Trang Bang District, Subregion 1, indicates that a total of 1,000 "suspects" have been investigated and classified in the district since the 1968 Tet Offensive.[45] Indeed, the documents convey the impression that the Viet Cong are investing an enormous effort in identifying and classifying persons who may be unsympathetic toward and potentially dangerous to their movement.

Recent data suggest that high priority continues to be given to the development of blacklists. A Secret security directive of May 18, 1969, attributed to a Viet Cong unit in Can Duoc District, Subregion 3, urged district and village security agents to "make out rosters of tyrants in each hamlet and village," including the "crimes committed by each wicked tyrant," so that each might be "duly punished." The directive went on to state:

All district security agents should consider that this is the most important point of the revolutionary task. In so doing, we will satisfactorily carry out the mission of exterminating the wicked tyrants, loosening the enemy grip, and maintaining security which will counter enemy spying activities.[46]

4

The Forms of Repression

In some respects, the methods of repression employed by the Viet Cong are dictated by the security status of the areas in which the targets reside. Where the GVN's presence is dominant, assassinations and abductions are the major forms of repression. In areas under Viet Cong control and those where the Communist infrastructure is relatively free from GVN harassment, repression takes many different forms—from relatively mild disciplinary measures to such severe punishments as extended confinement in thought-reform camps and even execution. The following discussion, therefore, will treat the two kinds of territory separately. But it should be understood that the security situation in a given area of Vietnam may fluctuate markedly within a very short period.

Repression in GVN Areas:
Assassinations and Abductions

In GVN-controlled areas, or in those contested areas where the government's presence is strong, repressive measures mostly take the form of abduction or assassination. Persons who are abducted are moved into Viet Cong areas, where they are interrogated by security service cadres and, depending on the severity of their "crimes," may be released after a period of indoctrination, placed in detention camps, or executed.

Aside from such physical repression, the Viet Cong also conduct an extensive campaign to intimidate or subvert government personnel in GVN-controlled areas by issuing various forms of "warnings" (letters written to individual targets, messages passed through relatives, etc.). Through such communications, individuals are advised that they have been marked down for repression and that, unless they accommodate themselves to the Viet Cong (by resigning their positions or cooperating with the Front as fifth-columnists or intelligence agents), the repression will be consummated.

Available evidence suggests that the incidence of such warnings is quite large, and that for every GVN official or employee actually assassinated or kidnapped in some area several may only be warned. More will be said in Chapter 5 about the role of such warnings in the over-all Viet Cong plan. They constitute an important supplement to assassinations and abductions, and these severe punitive measures naturally serve to enhance the credibility of the warnings.

Assassinations and abductions have been an integral part of Communist operations in South Vietnam since the late 1950s; the years 1958 and 1959 alone witnessed an estimated 1,000 cases.[1] Prior to mid-1966, the absence of systematic procedures for collecting statistics on these events in the South (in many cases no count was kept by local authorities) leaves considerable uncertainty as to the actual number of assassinations and abductions between 1958 and 1965. However, according to figures released by the U.S. Mission in Saigon, the total for this eight-year period probably is around 46,500 of which some 9,700 were assassinations and the remaining 36,800 were listed as kidnappings. While noting that figures were "not entirely accurate," the Mission believed that any error was probably on "the low side."[2]

More reliable data, *although still incomplete,* are available from mid-1966 on. According to the statistics of the U.S. Mission, almost 44,000 persons were assassinated or abducted between January 1966 and the end of 1969.[3] Slightly more than 4,000 of these victims were reported to be government officials or employees, while the remainder were classified as members of the "general populace" (See table, p. 44). However, these estimates probably significantly understate the actual number of assassinations and abductions; moreover, the totals exclude all data for the month of February 1968 (the time of the Tet Offensive), when such activities appear to have been commonplace.

It will be noted that the table shows 1,817 government officials as having been assassinated or abducted during the four-year period in question. While this total includes titled officials from the national and corps levels down through province, district, and hamlet, the great bulk of the GVN persons so victimized were officials in villages and hamlets, more accessible to the Viet Cong's armed reconnaissance units than those at higher levels. It is estimated that village and hamlet leaders accounted for about 95 per cent of all officials assassinated or abducted during 1968 and 1969.[4]

The U.S. Mission also reported the abduction or assassination of 2,244 government employees, a category which includes various groups of civil servants (health workers, teachers, etc.), Rural

Development cadres, and members of the National Police (except those killed or captured while on military operations). The most frequent victims appeared to have been National Police personnel and Rural Development cadres. (In 1968 and 1969, for example, these two groups represented an estimated 85 per cent of all employees killed or kidnapped.[5]

Some 39,877 of the 43,938 persons reportedly assassinated or abducted between January 1966 and December 1969 were in the category of "general populace." In contrast to the figures given for government personnel, the number of abductions among the general populace far outweighed that of assassinations. Many civilians who are abducted apparently are held only for short periods of indoctrination and then are released. Many others are pressed into temporary service as porters for the Viet Cong and thereafter freed. Still others may be committed to more permanent service and used as replacements for local Viet Cong units.

A hundred or more civilians may be killed or kidnapped in a single Viet Cong raid on a village or refugee camp. For example, three Communist attacks in December 1967 accounted for almost one-quarter of the 2,651 civilians reported to have been abducted or killed during the last three months of 1967: 114 highlanders were massacred during an attack on the village of Dak Son in Phuoc Long Province, another 200 were kidnapped in Kontum Province, and some 300 refugees were abducted from a camp in Binh Dinh Province. The purpose of such attacks probably varies. It may be to recruit needed manpower. In some cases, the objective may be to deter villagers from seeking refuge in government areas; in others, to set an example by "punishing" a village that has cooperated too closely with the GVN.

Some of those killed may be collateral victims of Communist assassination attempts on other targets, as when a bomb is exploded in a restaurant or on a street corner in front of a government office.[6] But one must assume that a good number of those assassinated or abducted in this "general populace" category belong to specific target groups. Many probably are persons whom the Viet Cong believe to be GVN spies or informants. Some no doubt are political party members, ralliers, or former government officials; some are on blacklists for being closely associated with the GVN ("collaborators").[7] And we know from captured documents that the relatives and dependents of government persons also may become targets for assassination or abduction.[8]

U.S. Mission Reports of
Assassinations and Abductions,
1966-1969[a]

	1966		1967		1968[b]		1969		1966-1969[b]	
	Assassinations	Abductions	Assassinations	Abductions	Assassinations	Abductions	Assassinations	Abductions	Assassinations	Abductions
Government Officials[c]	168	176	285	192	364	183	336	113	1,153	664
Government Employees[d]	202	93	603	136	611	118	447	34	1,863	381
General Populace	1,362	3,541	2,818	5,041	5,543	10,332	5,292	5,948	15,015	24,862
Totals	1,732	3,810	3,706	5,369	6,518	10,633	6,075	6,095	18,031	25,907
	5,542		9,075		17,151		12,170		43,938	

[a]Since July 1968, data on assassinations and abductions have been reported as part of the Terrorist Incident Reporting System (TIRS) published by the Public Safety Division, MACCORDS in Saigon.

[b]These figures do not include any assassinations or abductions that may have occurred during February 1968. Official data for that month are not available.

[c]Includes titled officials at national, corps, region, province, district, village, and hamlet levels.

[d]Includes civil servants (teachers, health workers, etc.), Rural Development workers, and members of the National Police when not on military operations.

Impressive as the above numbers may appear, however, it is probable, as we have said, that they significantly understate the total number of GVN employees and others who were abducted or assassinated in those four years. There are several reasons for this. In the first place, under the reporting system employed by the U.S. Mission until July 1968, large numbers of victims apparently were simply omitted. It is possible that the official figures represented only about 60 per cent of the GVN officials and employees and other citizens actually involved. Even with the more accurate reporting system instituted in July 1968, the number of GVN officials and civil servants reported killed probably is substantially below the actual toll. This is due to the narrow reporting criteria of the U.S. Mission, which excludes the large numbers of GVN officials and employees killed as a result of military attacks and all other actions that are not considered assassinations. Between March and September 1968, for example, only a third of the National Police and Revolutionary Development cadres killed by the Viet Cong were reported as assassinations. The exclusion of GVN persons killed as the result of such enemy activity is often unwarranted and misleading, as the elimination of government officials and employees is among the principal objectives of many of the Viet Cong's military and paramilitary operations against GVN facilities. Assassination teams often operate in conjunction with other Viet Cong military units (such as a guerrilla squad or local force company) when attacking targets which possess any appreciable capacity for self-defense, such as police posts, the armed Revolutionary Development teams, and province and district headquarters. The Tet Offensive provided numerous instances of coordinated operations aimed at the annihilation of GVN officials in towns and cities.

The Tet Offensive and Hue

As mentioned earlier, the U.S. Mission provides no data on assassinations and abductions for the period of the Tet Offensive; official data for February 1968 simply are not available. But it is clear from the captured documents that the elimination of GVN officials, military leaders, spies, police, and other security elements was one of the principal objectives of the offensive.

During the attacks on Saigon, for example, a number of assassinations were planned and attempted against key GVN leaders as part of an over-all effort to repress "antirevolutionary personnel." A security report of February 27, 1968, attributed to the Security Section of the Saigon-Cholon-Gia Dinh Military Region revealed that according to "the general plan approved by the Party committee in December 1967" local security elements were to "coordinate with military units and youths to assassinate key [GVN] leaders" and to suppress "main [GVN] offices and oppressive agencies."[9] Security forces were directed to draw upon previously prepared blacklists and were to aim at GVN persons at all levels—"high, intermediate, and elementary"—in the mission described as the "suppression of antirevolutionary personnel":

This [Mission] is to be performed by security forces who will refer to the list of personnel already investigated, including personnel of high, intermediate, and elementary levels, spies, secret agents and reactionary factions. Key cadres should motivate the people on a broad front to participate in this activity.[10]

Among the leaders targeted for assassination were President Nguyen Van Thieu, General Nguyen Ngoc Loan (Director General of the National Police), General Linh Quang Vien (head of the Central Intelligence Organization), and Lieutenant Colonel Nguyen Van Luan (another important police official). One assassination team was assigned to killing Ambassador Ellsworth Bunker. For a variety of reasons, all these assassination attempts miscarried. According to the captured report, however, some of the teams assigned to eliminating these officials were able instead to reach other targets. For example, the "unit responsible for liquidating" President Thieu claimed to have "killed a number of public security agents, policemen, and Military Security Service (MSS) agents." The unit which had failed to mount the planned attack on General Vien's residence "was reassigned the mission of suppressing 'traitors' and succeeded in killing nearly 20 [GVN] public security and MSS agents" in the 6th precinct of Saigon and "a few others in the 2d and 5th precincts." The report also claims that Security Service cadres who had been assigned to help other Communist military units in the Saigon area "also captured more than 50 spies, public security, and MSS agents."[11]

Though it is impossible to estimate the total number of persons killed or abducted during the Tet Offensive in both urban and rural areas, it was certainly substantial. By Communist as well as Allied estimates, as many as three thousand persons may have been involved in the city of Hue and its environs alone. Hue was unique during the

Tet Offensive in being the one urban area which the Communists were able to hold for any appreciable length of time. On January 31, Communist regular forces, comprising some eight battalions (both Viet Cong and North Vietnamese), successfully infiltrated Hue "with the help of accomplices inside" and quickly gained control of most of the city.[12] These Communist units were later reinforced, and only after the bitterest fighting were U.S. and GVN forces able to regain full control of the city, when the last enemy remnants were routed from the imperial citadel on February 25.

In the intervening twenty-five days, despite fierce Allied counterattacks, Communist forces apparently had time and sufficient control to track down and eliminate hundreds of local GVN officials, administrative personnel, police, spies, political party members, and other target groups. There can be little doubt that the repression of such persons was one of their foremost objectives; captured notes, taken during a Party committee meeting in preparation for the Hue offensive, listed the "puppet administration" as one of the primary targets of the attack and suggested that the Communists intended to retain control of the city at least for a time.[13] Other enemy documents also explicitly state that one of the major missions of the campaign in Hue was to foment a general uprising, destroy "puppet" authorities and administrative agencies at all levels, and establish a "revolutionary administration" in the city.[14] There can be no doubt that a systematic attempt was made to root out such targets once Hue had been seized. A report marked "Absolute Secret," which covered Communist activities in the Hue area from January 31 to March 23, 1968, contained the following statement:

The people joined our soldiers in their search for tyrants, reactionaries and spies. For instance, Mrs. Xuan followed our soldiers to show the houses of the tyrants she knew, although she had only six days before giving birth to a child.[15]

Targets were also located with the aid of previously prepared blacklists and through the interrogation or cooperation of GVN personnel who were taken prisoner. According to a tape recording, for example, a company executive officer of the National Police Field Forces assisted the Viet Cong in tracking down GVN officials during the occupation.[16]

While a number of "special action" and "self-defense" units were apparently heavily involved in the mission of repressing GVN personnel,[17] attacking Main Force units also played a role in the capture and liquidation of "tyrants." An after-action report prepared by the commander of the 6th Regiment (Tri-Thien-Hue Military Region) on March 30, 1968, states that "various units" of the regiment were "coordinated with local troops to exterminate cruel tyrants and motivate the people to rise up inside and outside the citadel." According to this report, these forces along with "special action units and armed public security units" captured thousands of "local [GVN] administrative personnel, puppet troops, and cruel tyrants" and successfully annihilated members of "various reactionary political parties, henchmen, and wicked tyrants."[18]

Communist estimates of the number of persons killed in the Hue area tend to suggest, or support, a figure of about three thousand. One of the regiments involved in the attack, according to the above after-action report, claimed that its units alone, with the help of local agents, "killed 1,000 local administrative personnel, spies and cruel tyrants."[19] Another document, containing a report which the Tri-Thien-Hue Military Region had sent to North Vietnam, said that there were 2,867 persons killed in Hue City.[20] A captured notebook of an unidentified military cadre who had operated in the Hue area spoke of an "enormous victory" in which "more than 3,000 RVN personnel, including the Deputy Thua Thien Province chief, were killed." It went on to say:

The entire puppet administrative system from hamlet to province was destroyed or disintegrated. More than 3,000 persons were killed. The enemy could never reorganize or make up for his failure. Although he could immediately use inexperienced elements as replacements, they were good for nothing.[21]

Another Communist document, an activity report marked "Absolute Secret," also claimed a high toll (including many political party members) in the Hue area, reporting that in Huong Thuy District, immediately adjoining Hue City, for example, 670 "puppet authorities" had surrendered and that

We also killed one member of [the] Dai Viet Party Committee, one senator of South Vietnam, 50 Quoc Dan Dang Party [VNQDD] members, six Dai Viet Party members, 13 Can Lao Nhan Vi Party members, three captains, four first lieutenants, and liberated 35 hamlets with 32,000 people.

In the adjoining district of Phu Vang,

We eliminated 1,892 administrative personnel, 38 policemen, 790 tyrants, six captains, two first lieutenants, 20 second lieutenants, and many NCOs.[22]

The document also reported the capture in Phu Vang of six members of the Dai Viet Party (including one member of its region committee and an official of the Central Committee), and of three VNQDD members (including a member of the Nam Bo Party Committee).[23] While one must be cautious in accepting detailed Communist claims such as these and must allow for some element of exaggeration, they nevertheless suggest the relative scale and intensity of repression in the Hue area.

In trying to arrive at an objectively accurate picture, one does not have to rely on Communist figures alone. The successive discovery of mass graves in the Hue area during the months since the Tet Offensive has yielded an ever clearer picture of the number of persons murdered by the Communists. Estimates of the total number killed have mounted with each new discovery. In April 1968, for example, the U.S. Mission initially reported that about one thousand South Vietnamese government workers and other civilians were executed in Hue during the Lunar New Year offensive. This report—which was based on a joint investigation by American and South Vietnamese authorities—revealed that several hundred victims had been found buried in nineteen mass graves in the Hue area. "Evidence indicated that many victims had been beaten to death, shot, beheaded or buried alive" and "many bodies were found bound together in groups of 10 or 15, eyes open, with dirt or cloth stuffed in their mouths."[24]

Some of the uncovered bodies had bullet wounds. A Buddhist monk in a nearby pagoda was said to have reported hearing "nightly executions by pistol and rifle shots in a plowed field behind the pagoda during the first two weeks of February, with victims pleading for mercy." However, nearly half the bodies uncovered in the graves "were found in conditions indicating that they had been buried alive." One such victim was an 80-year-old teacher, who had been buried alive because he was "accused of having a son in the army." Several cadavers had also been beheaded. Many of the men and women who had been executed appeared "to be government employees or citizens linked to the South Vietnamese regime"; one of the victims was identified as a prominent leader of the VNQDD. However, some of those killed were non-Vietnamese, including several French priests and four German faculty members of the Hue University medical school.[25]

In the year-and-a-half since the Tet Offensive, the discovery of mass graves has continued to be a common occurrence. According to a May 1969 news report of a mass burial in Hue City, fewer than half the bodies recovered had been identified, but many were thought to be "South Vietnamese soldiers and minor government officials." Allied authorities reportedly believed that the names of many of the victims had appeared on Communist blacklists, but they could not account for some of the murdered women and children. Many of the newly-discovered graves, like those exhumed earlier, contained victims who had been buried alive or beaten to death. In one skeleton, every principal bone was found to have been broken.[26]

By late 1969, the total number of bodies unearthed around Hue had risen to about 2,800. These actual counts would seem to lend credibility to Communist claims that about three thousand persons were eliminated during the occupation of Hue. It is possible that the final figure will be even higher, for many are still reported as missing. Whatever the true number may turn out to be, it was sizable for a city with a population of a little more than 150,000.

The savagery and indiscriminate nature of much of the repression in Hue seemed uncharacteristic of the Viet Cong's Security Service. It is possible that some of the more brutal killings were not carried out by security cadres at all but were performed by the North Vietnamese or other military forces. Indeed, according to an activity report produced by the Security Section of Quang Tri Province on April 10, 1968, and apparently addressed to the Security Section of the Tri-Thien-Hue Military Region, many security cadres "questioned" the mass assassinations of GVN and RVNAF persons who had *surrendered* to the Communists in Hue; these cadres believed that such mass assassinations were inconsistent with Viet Cong policy, but understood that the Region had nothing to say about it.[27] In some instances troop discipline may have broken down under the pressure of the heavy fighting. The notebook of a cadre who participated in the battles in and around Hue reported that the troops "were afraid of being discovered by the enemy" and that "it was very difficult for them to handle POWs, so they executed [a] policy of 'catch and kill'."[28]

Whatever misgivings some cadres may have had about the practice in Hue, however, the Communists looked upon the repression in that city as both necessary and generally successful. In the words of one classified activity report, "Hue was the place where reactionary spirit had existed for over ten years. However, it only took us a short time to drain it to its root."[29]

Indeed, there is even evidence to suggest that at least some

Communist officials considered the primary shortcoming of the repression in Hue to have been that it did not go far enough. According to a December 1968 report attributed to the Hue City Party Committee, too many "tyrants" were spared during the 25-day occupation. While noting that "thousands of tyrants were killed" and that "many reactionary factions and organizations were exterminated," the critique listed among the major "defects" of the Hue campaign the fact that "the reactionary organizations" had not been "tracked down to the last" and that a "number of traitorous Vietnamese and tyrants had been released." Said the report:

In some places, the motivation of the masses to rise up and seize power was carried out slowly, and not completely. Therefore, the reactionary organizations and agencies of the enemy were not tracked down to the last. In other places, the working-class viewpoint was not firm, that was why a certain number of traitorous Vietnamese and tyrants had been released . . . and thus difficulties were created for the Movement. [30]

The Armed Reconnaissance Units

Prior to the Tet Offensive, primary responsibility for assassinations and abductions in GVN-controlled areas rested with the specially-trained Armed Reconnaissance Units, which the Viet Cong have established at various echelons of their Security Service. Believed to exist at the region, subregion, province, town, district, and village levels of the security apparatus, these units are administratively part of the Espionage Subsections of their parent Security Sections. In the past, most Armed Reconnaissance Units were relatively small. In 1965, for example, a six-man team would be attached to the Espionage Subsection of each provincial Security Section, and a three to five-man squad to the Espionage Subsection of the district organization.[31] However, there is reason to believe that the units have been enlarged in recent years.[32] The Viet Cong also have formed Armed Reconnaissance cells in some villages, and have deployed "armed security agents" even at the hamlet level.[33] These elements participate in the repression of targets and cooperate with Communist regular or paramilitary units in carrying out raids in their local areas.

The mission of the Armed Reconnaissance Units is primarily the assassination and abduction of GVN personnel, but it also includes the capture of government documents for intelligence exploitation.

In explaining their role in province capitals, cities, and towns, a Region II security directive said that their "main mission" was to

... eliminate traitors and tyrants [so as] to break the enemy's control; create a political problem in his ranks; capture the enemy ... for exploitation and attack the overt and covert objectives to seize important documents. The main objectives to be exterminated by the Armed Reconnaissance [Units] are the heads and the wicked tyrants of the oppressive, counterespionage, intelligence and reactionary organizations and the agencies and headquarters of the same.[34]

The operations of these units are in many cases highly professional. The targets, who are selected from existing blacklists, are usually reconnoitered thoroughly before being hit. Where a target is well protected, local Reconnaissance Units may recruit additional military personnel to assist in them. For less complicated jobs and readily accessible targets, the Security Service will sometimes employ local thugs or even children to carry out assassinations.

Targets may be sentenced to death in absentia before being assassinated. Among examples of this practice was the case of six GVN persons who were issued death sentences for "counterrevolutionary activities" by the "Tay Ninh Province Liberation Army" between April 28 and May 19, 1967. They were: a commander of a GVN outpost, a policeman, an assistant leader of a GVN youth organization, two CIDG members stationed at a local watchtower, and a CIDG platoon leader who had been a Viet Cong cadre before surrendering to the government.[35] Another set of captured verdicts, issued by the "Phu Cat District People's Court" in Binh Dinh Province on September 19, 1968, pronounced death sentences on the following persons in a single village, and directed local units to carry them out: a policeman from Phu Cat District; the chairman of the Dai An Village Administrative Council; a policeman from Dai An Village; a security agent; and a hamlet chief.[36]

Some indication of the professionalism and careful preparation which characterize many Armed Reconnaissance operations can be garnered from the specialized training that these units receive. Several captured documents which the Viet Cong have produced for instructional purposes reveal some of the content and scope of this training.[37] The topics covered in these training materials include the problems that are peculiar to operating in towns and cities (such as the problem of maintaining security and concealment), the various kinds of reconnaissance required in planning assassination missions (techniques for investigating and shadowing targets), the methods of assassination, and stratagems for escape once a mission is accomplished.

One training document, entitled "The Task of Breaking the Enemy Control and Eliminating the Tyrants in the City," emphasized such topics as the weapons to be used, the personnel requirements for different assassination missions, the basic information needed in planning a mission, and the individual assignments for each team member during the three phases of the assassination operation—approach, attack, and retreat.[38]

The document also specified three alternative settings for assassinations: "We can kill a person at his own house or at his office . . . . We can kill him when he is going to work or on his way home from his office, when he is riding a bicycle or driving a car. We can lure him into a love trap or kill him during a party."[39]

Like other training materials, this document laid heavy stress on the need for meticulous preparation. Plans for all assassination missions were to be based on a detailed investigation of the target, including his habits and patterns of movement, and a thorough reconnoitering of his residence and place of work. Among the details to be established were the kinds of visitors the target normally received at home, the times and places where he ate and slept, the vehicles and streets by which he traveled to work, the clothes he wore, and any interests he might have such as "prostitutes, music, dancing, movies, sports, bicycle racing, wine, or opium." In carrying out their individual assignments, the document said, team members "must be determined and act bravely without hesitation or mercy." Heavy emphasis was given to the successful accomplishment of the mission: "If we meet the enemy [we must] try to execute him at once; we will pass up an opportunity if we don't kill him."[40]

The "Suicide Cell" and Other Repressive Instruments

With the initiation of the General Offensive and General Uprising in 1968, the Viet Cong departed from their previous practice of entrusting assassination in GVN-controlled areas mainly to the specialized Armed Reconnaissance Teams, by assigning this mission to newly-formed security components (the "Armed Security Forces") and also to many of the regular combat units. The principal reason for this policy change was the prospect that the opportunities and requirements for repression in the General Offensive phase would far exceed the capabilities of the existing reconnaissance units. By attacking a number of cities, towns, and villages simultaneously, the Viet Cong expected to have immediate access to a large number of targets, and since a main purpose of the attacks was to disintegrate GVN control, additional forces had to be recruited to handle repression. Among those newly assigned to this mission were village and "secret" guerrilla units, district and provincial forces, and even regular NVA units. A few examples of the documentary evidence will convey the picture:

— A notebook captured in July 1968 and attributed to a cadre of the 1st Regiment, Subregion 4, stated that soldiers from the Regiment would "join the local people in oppressing the reactionary elements and administrative personnel of the enemy."[41]

— A circular dated September 4, 1968, attributed to the Current Affairs Committee of the Bien Hoa Province Unit directed that, in towns and cities, special action units, secret guerrilla members, and armed security agents were to concentrate their efforts on annihilating GVN policemen, tyrants, and chiefs of city wards during the climaxing phase of the General Uprising. Armed propaganda elements were also ordered to eliminate tyrants.[42]

— A notebook with entries dated between November 1967 and April 1968, maintained by a cadre in charge of guerrilla and local forces in Thua Thien Province, revealed that the mission of guerrilla and district units in the Province included the assassination of GVN local administrative and intelligence personnel.[43]

— A notebook maintained by a member of a company-size unit subordinate to a regiment in the Tri-Thien-Hue Military Region stated that, as part of its mission, the unit had to completely annihilate "tyrants" in its area of responsibility during the period from mid-April to the end of July 1968.[44]

— A notebook attributed to a member of the 4th Battalion, Quyet

Thang Regiment, 3rd NVA Division, contained an entry dated March 1968, stating that the mission of the battalion included coordinating efforts with local force elements to suppress GVN administrative officials and informers.[45]

Numerous captured directives revealed that various regular and paramilitary units were ordered to kill "tyrants," hamlet officials, or pacification cadres; to destroy "oppressing elements and reactionary organizations"; or to "intimidate the negative" [uncooperative civilians].[46]

In addition to calling upon the types of combat units described above, the Viet Cong decided to augment its repressive machinery for the General Offensive with an entirely new unit: the "suicide cell." In November 1967, a series of directives were issued by provincial authorities calling upon subordinate organizations to form three-man suicide cells for the purpose of suppressing "tyrants," "spies," and pacification personnel so as to help the populace break the enemy's control.[47] These cells were organized mainly at the village level and often consisted of teenagers.[48] In one district of Binh Dinh Province, for example, each village was ordered to establish a suicide unit of ten to twenty male and female members, 15 years or older, and to organize this unit into three-man cells. Their stated mission was to annihilate the Biet Kich (Special Forces), "traitors," and Rural Development cadres in their own area, and also to penetrate deeply into GVN rear areas so as to be able to attack key posts and billets of enemy commanders, "tyrants," and pacification personnel, with a view to breaking enemy pressure and liberating the rural areas.[49]

The Viet Cong apparently hoped that these teenage cells would set an example to all the villagers and cause them to rise up and overthrow the local GVN administration. A letter dated November 1, 1967, and attributed to the Secretary of the Ban Me Thuot Province Party Committee directed that suicide cells be activated for the specific mission of killing "wicked tyrants in hamlets and villages." Its instructions were specific:

... each hamlet where our agents are available should choose from 2 to 3 persons to activate a hamlet uprising section and 2 to 3 suicide cells (selected from among male and female youths) to keep track of and to destroy wicked tyrants in [the] hamlet. ... At present, the conditions are ripe for the implementation of the plan of the Revolution; however [the] people are controlled by wicked tyrants and administrative personnel in hamlets and villages. If we are able to guide suicide units to kill these wicked tyrants, the people in villages and hamlets, even though there are no agents present, will rise up to overthrow the enemy government and support and join the Revolution.[50]

The employment of suicide cells seems to have continued throughout the various stages of the General Offensive, as there are references to them in captured documents produced as late as August 1968.[51] One such document, dated August 8, concerned preparations for the Third General Offensive in Quang Ngai Province. It directed all Party Committees and Military Command Committees in one district to

... urgently establish "suicide teams," swear them in and prepare to infiltrate them into towns to assassinate tyrants and ringleaders in order to effectively support the destruction of the enemy's control... and create favorable conditions for the masses to rise up. Each village must establish at least a three-man suicide cell, preferably all Party or Group members, who will be equipped with light weapons such as two grenades, daggers. . . . These people should be ready to go upon order.[52]

The creation of suicide cells and the widespread involvement of both regular and guerrilla forces in the capture and liquidation of "tyrants" have resulted in a significant "deprofessionalization" of the Communists' repressive machinery in the South. Such units are undoubtedly less disciplined and discerning in their conduct than are the highly trained and specialized Security Service units and, as a result, are more prone to the excesses which the Communists have long considered impolitic. One must assume that the Communist leadership, in enlisting these units in the repressive mission, was aware of this danger, but accepted the political risk as necessary to bringing about the rapid disintegration of the GVN.

Repression in Viet Cong Areas

In areas actually under Viet Cong control and those where the Communist infrastructure is comparatively free from GVN harassment, the forms of repression are much more varied. A continuum of increasingly severe punitive measures ranges from such relatively mild disciplinary actions as "warnings," "in-place reform" (compulsory indoctrination), and home surveillance for minor offenders to the severest forms of punishment: extended confinement to hard labor in "thought-reform" camps, and execution.

The rationale for such a graduated arsenal of repressive measures is derived in part from doctrinal considerations; in part it is a matter of expediency. The Viet Cong place heavy emphasis on the desirability of "reforming" those who may transgress against the Revolution, and of accomplishing this rehabilitation with no more than the degree of coercion necessary; their doctrine also stresses that the "punishment should fit the crime." Both these considerations, therefore, call for a rather flexible array of repressive measures. Furthermore, in areas held by the Communists, repression often serves as a form of "population control": as a way of coercing laggards or malcontents; of punishing minor infractions of local regulations; and of regulating and reforming errant attitudes toward the Revolution. As such deviant behavior and attitudes are not uncommon in VC-controlled areas, disciplinary mechanisms must be capable of accommodating sizable numbers of people. Much of this reform has to be accomplished within the society of village and hamlet, for, if the Viet Cong were to attempt to arrest all doubters and critics, their numbers would rapidly exceed the capacity of the detention facilities. In discussing the problem of reforming the many persons who had "previously worked for the enemy," one directive said: "Since we cannot kill or put them all in prison, we find an alternate way of dealing with them."[53]

Although the major focus of this paper is on the more severe forms of repression, the milder kind deserve brief mention; they are the warning, in-place reform (compulsory indoctrination), home surveillance, and reduction in prestige.

Warning

The mildest and probably most common form of repression is the warning, whereby an individual is formally notified that his deviant behavior or attitude has come to the attention of local security cadres and that it must be rectified. In the words of a Region II directive, the warning is "applied to enemy elements who do not deserve to be put under surveillance or arrest," and its aim is to prevent misdemeanants from "going deeper into crime" and to "make them become honest people." It is intended to demonstrate both the "strict viewpoint" and the "tolerance of the Revolution." In liberated areas according to the directive, "warnings can be implemented by many methods":

Pay a call on the objectives for indoctrination; warn and make them write a self-criticism report. Make them acknowledge all crimes and promise never to commit them again and ask for the sponsorship of their families. In some cases, the security agencies will just warn them and let their families assume the work of indoctrination. We can also send them to the hamlet and village so they can acknowledge their crimes to the people and promise never to commit them again and then let their families indoctrinate them.[54]

The above passage points up several characteristics which most of the milder forms of repression seem to have in common. The target is required to make a formal acknowledgment of his crimes; his family may be held responsible for his indoctrination and subsequent behavior; and he may be forced to recant his crimes before his fellow villagers.

In-Place Reform

In-place reform involves the compulsory attendance of indoctrination sessions organized by security cadres at the village level. These "concentrated reform courses" usually last from three to seven days, during which the subjects are required to "make a self-critique report in which they confess all the crimes"; "promise to correct them and never repeat them"; and vow never to "work as enemy lackeys again or cause damage to the Revolution and the people." Following their reform, the targets often are required to confess and denounce their past errors before their fellow villagers. Then they are released to their families, who "take them back home for continued indoctrination."[55]

The purpose of in-place reform is to "make a clean sweep of reactionary ideologies" and change "antirevolutionary elements into honest people" so that they will "participate in the struggle against the American imperialists and their henchmen for the liberation of South Vietnam."[56] To determine whether an individual has been successfully reformed or whether more severe action is indicated, the Viet Cong apply several criteria, among them the "faithful confession of all crimes"; willingness to denounce others "who are secretly operating for the enemy"; readiness to fully execute all "guidelines and policies of the Party" including the implementation of "various missions in the local areas"; and willingness to "strictly comply with all regulations [concerning] counterespionage and security maintenance."[57]

According to captured directives, the categories of persons who may be subject to in-place reform are "those who previously were enemy henchmen" (such as former GVN administrative personnel and members of reactionary parties); "individuals who are working for the enemy" but who "are not yet worth being arrested"; "dissatisfied elements, whose activities are harmful to the Revolution"; the families of "exiled elements" (those who have fled to GVN-controlled areas); and "the families whose relatives have been severely punished" by the Viet Cong.[58]

In some instances, people may be assigned to compulsory indoctrination courses for relatively minor offenses. A captured quarterly report from a village security agency, for example, revealed the crimes of "ten complicated elements" who had been forced to attend a seven-day reform course in the village: two female cadres who had committed adultery; two persons who had "insulted cadres"; and six persons who failed to "report to higher level when carrying wood" from the village.[59]

Home Surveillance

A somewhat more stringent form of repression is what the Viet Cong call "home surveillance." Under this procedure, subjects are confined to a specified area (usually their hamlet or village) for a set period of time and are kept under constant observation by other villagers or local security cadres. They are also required to undergo "reform," make public confession of their "crimes," and regularly present themselves (usually every two weeks) before their village Security Section to report on the progress of their reeducation. On occasion, they may also be required to perform labor tasks for the Viet Cong in order to "redeem" themselves. Periods of home surveillance can last from as little as six months to as much as two years, depending on the degree of the subject's guilt and the progress of his "reeducation."[60] A Region II security directive emphasized this flexibility as follows:

When the time of surveillance is over and if the subjects show some progress, we should release the control of them. If [they] still fail to improve, the time of surveillance can be extended. If, on the second time, the subjects have still not improved, apply appropriate forms of oppression for punishment. However, there are some special cases where the subjects make much progress and naturally we can shorten the respective time of surveillance.[61]

Among persons subject to home surveillance, according to a MACV summary, are "those who are guilty of abusing the people but whose detention for a long period of time is not beneficial to the Revolution"; "those who are guilty of abusing the people but [who] have repented"; "hooligans"; and "those who have been freed from a detention camp but who have not sincerely repented."[62]

Reduction in Prestige

This special form of repression usually is reserved for local government officials whom the Viet Cong wish to debase before their fellow villagers and use as objects for denigrating the government's prestige. Its victims are brought before one or more "condemnation meetings" of assembled villagers, where they are forced to "declare their crimes," denounce the GVN, and proclaim their repentance.[63] They usually read from prepared confessions, which have been screened by security cadres. The villagers are encouraged to pass judgment on whether the confession offered reveals a man's full guilt or whether he has committed additional crimes that call for more severe punishment. In Vietnamese society, such reduction-in-prestige sessions, like the public confessions that are part of other types of repression, mentioned earlier, can be a cruel form of punishment, as for some people "extreme loss of face and public humiliation" constitute sanctions "only slightly less severe than death itself."[64]

Arrest, Thought Reform, and Execution

Persons suspected of more serious offenses, and those who fail to respond to the milder forms of repression described above, are arrested and placed under detention and, after a period of "investigation" (meaning, interrogation) by Security Service cadres, may be imprisoned in thought-reform camps or executed. Those for whom confinement in a camp does not seem warranted are returned to their home villages for appropriate reform.

The targets as well as the purpose of arrest are described in the 1967 security directive from Region II:

. . . arrest is a form of oppression applied [to] reactionary elements who have committed serious crimes towards the people and the Revolution. This aims at depriving [them of] their right to live freely in the society; prevents them from causing difficulties and damage to the Revolution; wears down and disintegrates the enemy, and at the same time motivates the people to fight against spies and reactionaries.[65]

The statement that only "serious crimes" warrant arrest must be read in light of the very broad construction that the Viet Cong tend to place on what constitutes a serious offense. Actually, arrests have been quite common in past years, numbering some 800 to 900 a year in some provinces. They include many persons whose only "crime" is to have a close relative working for the GVN or who manifest a lack of sympathy for the Revolution. This is illustrated by a captured roster of 685 individuals arrested by the Viet Cong in seven villages of the Duc Pho District, Quang Ngai Province, from 1965 to early 1967. The roster, while it included many local government officials, suspected "spies" and intelligence agents, policemen, and members of various GVN military and paramilitary forces (ARVN, Civil Guard, Popular Force, etc.), also contained many persons whose crimes were summed up in the following notations: "distorting Communism"; "sympathizing" with the enemy; "spreading rumors to belittle"; "spoke evil of" or "attacked revolutionary policy"; "opposing the denunciation campaign"; "opposed cadre"; "escapist who neglected his missions [and] resisted local cadre"; "wife of an enemy soldier"; "husband is an enemy tyrant"; "his son joined the enemy army"; and so forth.[66]

Some persons who are arrested are the victims of personal vendettas with local Viet Cong cadres, as was borne out by a high-level security directive, captured in 1966, which complained that persons were being detained without adequate cause and that some cadres had detained honest inhabitants for reasons of personal vengeance.[67]

Once arrested, the victims undergo an "investigation" (based in part on information contained in the blacklists but also on subsequent interrogation by security cadres) to establish the magnitude of their crimes and the sentences to be imposed. The more important "tyrants," and persons who might be profitably exploited for intelligence information, are often sent to higher echelons (province or above) for processing, while military prisoners usually are turned over to military channels and interrogated by the Viet Cong military intelligence and military proselytizing agencies.

At the district level, responsibility for the processing of the prisoners rests with the interrogation and detention element of the Internal Security Subsection of the district security organization; at province level and above, with the Legal Affairs Subsections that are organized at the several echelons of the security apparatus. In the course of his interrogation, a subject must provide a full personal history statement, confess all his "crimes," and denounce any other persons who might be "secretly operating for the enemy" (that is to say, he has to assist in the development of additional blacklists). In the case of GVN military or paramilitary personnel, such confessions typically include any operations in which their units committed such crimes against the people as "herding" the population into strategic hamlets, confiscating the people's rice, livestock, or material possessions, and burning or destroying their houses. For GVN administrative personnel, confession may cover a variety of activities, from the harassment or suppression of Viet Cong cadres to the collection of taxes for the GVN. In short, almost any pro-government or anti-Communist activity or attitude, whether or not it is performed or expressed in the course of official duties, may constitute a crime in Viet Cong eyes and thus become grist for confessions.

In interrogations, a high premium is placed on cooperation and veracity, and it goes very hard with those who attempt to dissemble or refuse to cooperate. This harsh policy was reflected in a letter about the transfer of seventeen prisoners to a provincial thought-reform camp, which recommended that the provincial authorities "investigate them further and take severe measures against any who are stubborn."[68] A Liberation Army directive concerning "Policy Toward Prisoners and Surrenderers" captured in August 1967 is more explicit:

Severity should be reserved for those who are stubborn and false in their statements and those who have acted against our orders or who have organized an escape. For punishment they will probably be detained in dark trenches and their daily ration will be reduced by one-half. In serious cases, they will possibly be shot.[69]

Even though torture is generally proscribed under Viet Cong policy, it nevertheless is sometimes employed during both investigation and detention. A major point of criticism in a directive captured in 1966 was that "torture" was being used against persons under detention. Another directive, attached to the first, mentioned that "torture may be used for thought reform only when this is requested by a majority of the people."[70]

Once an investigation has been completed, appropriate authorities determine whether the prisoner is to be released to his home village, to remain incarcerated, or to be executed.[71] In past years, authority to impose harsh sentences (execution or long-term imprisonment) was usually restricted to the higher levels (province and above) of the Viet Cong security and political bureaucracy. For example, a 1965 directive stated that the district echelon was allowed to pronounce sentences of one to three years of imprisonment, and the province, of three years or more (presumably, including death), but that for certain categories of prisoners—namely, "enemy ringleaders, chiefs of province, and officers ranking from major and higher"—only the Region Party Committee and Current Affairs Committee could pronounce sentences of death or imprisonment.[72] Another directive, from about the same period, states that the Province Party Committee and Current Affairs Committee have the authority to execute persons, but that they must make a report to higher echelons.[73]

With the inception of the General Offensive, however, and the concomitant intensification of the campaign against "tyrants" and "reactionaries," the Viet Cong were compelled, at least in some areas, to alter this policy and to grant authority for executions to much lower echelons. An activity report written in April 1968 by a security cadre in the Tri-Thien-Hue region stated that, "for the time being," death sentences for GVN officials and RVNAF personnel were to be pronounced by authorities at the village level in Thua Thien and Hue but by district authorities in Quang Tri Province.[74]

In a minority of cases, the accused receives a public trial in a People's Court before being sentenced. Most of those placed on trial are serious offenders (e.g., spies and "wicked" security agents), who are selected because they can serve as a warning to others, and many of them are given the death sentence. Thus, the People's Courts fulfill a useful psychological function—providing a deterrent to other GVN agents and a general object lesson for the public at large. Trials are staged at both provincial and district level, and in some instances appear to be conducted with all the trappings of a formal court of law, including the presence of a magistrate, a clerk, and even a defense counsel.

Thought-Reform Camps

Incarceration in thought-reform camps is a widely-employed form of repression, and there is strong evidence that many thousands of persons have been subjected to the rigors of hard labor and forced indoctrination in such camps over the past few years.

The Security Service is known to maintain detention facilities at region, province, and district levels. (Some villages also have rudimentary jails, but prisoners are seldom held in these lock-ups for more than a week or two.) The most important prisoners, such as senior officials, officers, and intelligence personnel, are probably held at the regional camps, but the vast majority of prisoners are detained in province and district facilities. The number of these facilities may vary from province to province, depending on the prevailing security status, but in general there seems to be at least one for each province (some provinces have two), which may hold up to 200 or more persons, and each district subordinate to the province has a separate detention camp holding anywhere from 25 to 100 or more prisoners. Camps are usually situated in remote areas and are garrisoned by detachments of Security Service troops which both guard the prisoners and attempt to provide sufficient protection for the camp to permit the evacuation of prisoners in the event of Allied sweep operations.

As a general rule, detention facilities maintained by the Security Service are not used for the run-of-the-mill ARVN prisoner captured in battle. The great majority of these military prisoners are sent to separate detention camps run by the Viet Cong's Military Proselytizing apparatus, where they undergo indoctrination aimed at recruiting them as fifth-columnists for the Viet Cong, and thereafter are often released.[75] However, those military prisoners who prove particularly "stubborn," or who hold positions in the ARVN which make them important targets for repression (such as officers and MSS or other intelligence personnel), or who after interrogation are adjudged to owe a particular "blood debt" to the Revolution are turned over to the security apparatus for detention and processing through its own channels.[76]

As a result, most prisoners in Security Service camps belong to such target groups as suspected or proven spies, GVN officials or local administrative personnel, members of the National Police, Chieu Hoi or Revolutionary Development cadres, Viet Cong deserters, and persons otherwise suspected of collaborating with the GVN. In addition, these camps are used to punish and reform "hostile" or "backward" civilians who refuse to cooperate with local

Viet Cong authorities or who prove "committed to their social class." Some idea of the variety of prisoners that a detention camp may hold can be gained from the following captured reports:

— A June 1967 report from a district detention camp in Quang Nam Province, which revealed a total prisoner population of 96 including 15 spies and informants, 25 reactionaries, 6 hamlet administrative personnel, 36 Chieu Hoi cadres, 4 collaborators, and 10 persons who had surrendered.[77]

— A quarterly activity report of Soc Trang Province dated March 1966, which disclosed that among the 205 persons arrested and detained in the province during the first quarter of 1966 were 19 policemen, 25 intelligence agents, 6 village and hamlet officials, 3 informers, 7 penetration agents, 5 landlords siding with the enemy, and 1 CIA agent.[78]

— A captured roster of 123 persons who had been imprisoned in a district detention camp in Phu Yen Province between 1965 and early 1967. Listed among the prisoners who had been detained for periods of from a few months to over two years were: 6 known enemy spies, 30 suspected spies, 15 village and hamlet administrative personnel, 17 "individuals in exile" (i.e., persons who had fled to GVN areas), 21 puppet soldiers (including 1 Regional Force officer and 1 Popular Force officer), 2 policemen, 2 Dai Viets, 2 persons in "contact with the band in exile," 3 deserters, 7 "backward civilians," 7 persons "committed to social abuses," 2 persons "committed to their social class," 2 guilty of "insubordination," 2 persons who stole food or property "meant for the Revolution," and 1 individual who had oppressed "persons who had participated in the Resistance."[79]

The period of confinement depends in the main on the severity of the person's alleged crime and the progress he makes in reorientation and labor activities while in camp. Formal sentences may run from as long as twenty years to as short as a few months. The width of the spectrum of penalties is illustrated by a security directive issued in December 1965, which states that a sentence of from ten to twenty years' imprisonment (or of death) could be meted out to those who "are consciously and actively operating against the Revolution," are "in blood debt to the people," or attempt to "spoil the revolutionary movement in different local areas." For those "enemy henchmen who are operating against the Revolution [but] whose crimes are light," sentences of ten years or less were indicated, a level of punishment deemed appropriate also for those who, having committed serious crimes, "are repenting about their past activities" and "show sincere contrition."[80]

For less serious offenses, the directive suggested sentencing culprits to three months of "forced and concentrated reorientation" in thought-reform camps, a sentence considered appropriate for those who had "collaborated with the enemy" and for persons who had committed crimes (including "relatively important crimes") but had "rallied to our cause." If warranted, an additional three months could be added to this sentence at the discretion of local authorities, but if, after one such extension, a person showed no sign of repentance, he was to be judged by the court.[81]

It is probable that a majority of those entering camps are detained for less than six months. Many of them either are serving brief sentences of the three-month kind or have never been formally sentenced at all. The latter group consists of the large numbers of individuals who are arrested as "suspects" and, after interrogation and a period of reorientation, are released to the jurisdiction of security authorities in their home villages.[82] However, even persons who eventually are found innocent may remain in a camp up to three months while their cases are being processed.

There are several reports of "tyrants," "spies" and security personnel who have received sentences of between five and ten years or more. Occasionally, this severe a sentence is given also to persons in other target categories, such as the clerk from a district Self-Defense Office who was sentenced to seven years' imprisonment, to be followed by two years of home surveillance.[83] But the evidence from captured documents would seem to indicate that the longer sentences (four years or more) are handed down in only a minority of cases.

Sentences of from one to three years, however, are not uncommon for most target groups and are imposed even for such "crimes" as attempting to flee to GVN-controlled areas or maintaining contact with close relatives connected with the GVN. Illustrations of the types of sentences meted out for particular crimes are found in a series of captured rosters from the Tuy Hoa I District thought-reform camp, in Phu Yen Province, which list the crimes and other background data of some 200 persons who were imprisoned there between September 1964 and September 1966. Aside from numerous spies or suspected spies (many of whom were political party members) and hamlet administrative personnel who received sentences ranging from 12 to 36 months, the rosters included a number of persons who had been apprehended while attempting to flee to GVN areas or were charged with "intending" to "escape to the enemy controlled area," and who received sentences of from 10 to 24 months. Also on the roster were a number of individuals who had been in contact with relatives residing in GVN areas or "working for the enemy"; they included an interfamily leader whose "son is now working for the enemy" (15 months), a woman whose husband was a hamlet chief in a "GVN-controlled area and who intended to join him" (12 months), and a woman with "two children working for the enemy" whom she often contacted without the permission of the village cadres (12 months).[84]

Several prisoners who had been charged with spying, according to the rosters, clearly appeared to be victims of guilt by association, as, for example, the owner of a "gambling den" frequented by two "tyrants" of the Self-Defense Forces who, because of these contacts, was suspected of "being a secret agent of the enemy" (18 months), and a girl who had "made friends" with an enemy spy and was thus herself suspect. Finally, there were those on the rosters who had been imprisoned because they refused to carry out their "revolutionary tasks" or manifested attitudes hostile to the Revolution. Among these were: a youth who had been sentenced for "throwing sticks and stones at one of our meetings"; a "decadent student" who "evaded revolutionary tasks" while the "people were digging trenches and building combat villages" (6 months plus one year of in-place reform); and a VNQDD member who "neither enthusiastically engaged in revolutionary tasks nor had confidence in the Revolution" (10 months plus one year of in-place reform).[85]

The total number of prisoners held at any one time in a Viet Cong province has been as high as 700 to 900 in past years. The following figures on prisoner holdings in the province and subordinate district camps were reported by the Security Sections of four Viet Cong provinces in the Delta at different times between December 1965 and June 1968:

Date	Province	Number Reported[86]
December 1965	Ca Mau	890
January 1966	Rach Gia	876
March 1966	Ba Xuyen	850
March 1966	Soc Trang	746
June 1968	Ca Mau	484

The turnover rate in the prisoner populations of at least some provinces seems to be high. One provincial Security Section, for example, reported the arrest and imprisonment of 958 persons, said to be mainly local GVN administrative personnel and "spies," during a two-year period (1964-1966), but the same province also reported the *release* of some 567 individuals from two province-level camps in the same period.[87] A substantial turnover rate is reflected in other Communist security reports as well, lending support to the view that many sentences are short.[88]

At best, life in a thought-reform camp is harsh. Prisoners are forced to perform heavy manual labor (digging defensive trenches, clearing forests, or scratching out plots for food cultivation), and there seems to be a high incidence of illness, including beriberi and cholera.[89] Those of frail health or serving long sentences may not survive. One province, for instance, reported that some 70 persons had died because of illness in its camps between 1964 and 1966.[90] Although Viet Cong regulations forbid it, prisoners are sometimes tortured or physically mistreated by their guards; those who refuse to perform their labor tasks or prove openly hostile are subject to execution. If a camp threatens to be overrun by an Allied sweep operation, the more important prisoners may be killed to ensure their not being liberated.[91] Prisoners caught attempting to escape usually are shot.

Since one of the principal purposes of incarceration is to "destroy antirevolutionary thoughts" and change the individual's ideological standpoint in favor of the Revolution,[92] prisoners are subjected to incessant reorientation sessions. The substance of this concentrated indoctrination includes lectures on such matters as the "nature of American aggression in Vietnam," the "criminal acts" of the "GVN puppets," the "just cause" of the Front, and the "certain victory" of the Revolution. Prisoners are required to participate in self-criticism sessions, fully confess all crimes, and demonstrate repentance. Some prisoners are forced to write propaganda tracts against the GVN in which they call upon their former colleagues to defect to the Viet

Cong. Those who refuse to do so are threatened with a cut in their rice rations or with being tried by a People's Court.[93] However, there is a considerable premium on cooperation, as the two principal criteria for release from detention seem to be the prisoner's relative "enthusiasm" for his labor tasks and his "evolution of ideology"—including, of course, a full confession of all guilt.[94]

Execution

According to Viet Cong doctrine, the ultimate and severest form of repression—execution—is reserved for those guilty of "serious" crimes against the Revolution; those who owe a clear "blood debt" to the people; those whose continued existence would constitute a threat to the Revolution; and those who are adjudged unregenerate (that is, beyond hope of redemption through thought reform). The categories of persons who are most commonly victims of capital punishment include spies, reactionary "ringleaders," individuals labeled as "cruel" or "wicked tyrants," and very "stubborn" elements who fail to respond to less stringent forms of repression or who refuse to cooperate during interrogation.

The security directive issued at the end of 1965 authorized long-term imprisonment or the death sentence for

those who are the enemy henchmen, are consciously and actively operating against the Revolution, and by their own will are in blood debt to the people or who try to spoil the revolutionary movement in different local areas.

More specifically,

The sentence of death is [to be] pronounced against those who initiated the criminal schemes or reactionary ringleaders whose crimes were serious, provoking indignation from the people, and [who] cannot be reoriented any more.[95]

Clearly, the criteria laid down for a sentence of capital punishment are rather broad, and allow Communist authorities considerable leeway in deciding whether to invoke it. Although individuals from all target groups are subject to execution, the major categories appear to be "spies" and other intelligence personnel, GVN officials, police and other security personnel, Viet Cong defectors, and leaders and members of certain political parties. According to one captured document, for example, all thirty persons put to death in a district of Binh Dinh Province in 1965 were GVN spies, security and police personnel, or local administrative authorities. They included two men in their seventies and several other persons of advanced years.[96]

A "Roster of Tyrants and Spies" produced by a district thought-reform camp in Phu Yen Province disclosed the "crimes" of some thirty-eight individuals who had been executed by local security cadres of the district, most of them during 1963 and 1964. Among those listed as having been either "killed on the spot" or "killed at detention camp" were several classes of spies ("hamlet," "village," "district," and "province" spies); "former" administrative personnel; "cruel" hamlet and interfamily chiefs; various "underground" village and district security agents; Dai Viet and Can Lao Party members; a "number one cruel village policeman"; an individual who had "left the liberated area" and who was "cruel and stubborn"; and a district agent who had "incited Catholics to counter the Revolution."[97] The roster also contained the names of numerous other "cruel" and "stubborn" tyrants and spies who had been "sentenced on the spot after an investigation" (which may mean that they, too, had been killed).

Other captured rosters and Security Service documents also frequently mention the execution of spies and other intelligence personnel, "security agents," and members of certain political parties, especially the VNQDD.[98] Occasionally, one also finds mention of CIDG members or rank-and-file military personnel, such as local self-defense-force members, who have been put to death.[99]

From the limited data available, it is not possible to arrive at a firm estimate of the number of persons the Viet Cong have executed in recent years. Such evidence as exists in the formal Security Service reports and detention-camp rosters would suggest that executions at the province, district, and village levels probably total, at the very least, several thousand a year. During 1965, for example, when enemy policy appeared to dictate that executions be "very limited," the Security Section of Rach Gia Province reported 40 death sentences in that province,[100] and Ca Mau Province reported 63 executions for the year.[101] To cite examples of executions at the district level, Huong Thuy District in Thua Thien Province reported 19 executions in 1965, while dossiers from Binh Khe District, Binh Dinh Province, indicate that at least 30 persons were put to death there during that year.[102] Executions are known to have occurred at the village level as well; the aforementioned Huong Thuy District, for example, reported that in 1965, 45 captives were sentenced to death in villages within its jurisdiction. Extrapolating from some of these reports, government analysts have estimated that the Viet Cong's 230-odd district Security Sections may execute as many as 5,000 persons a year, and that many more are put to death at province and village levels.

While data on the most recent years are somewhat sparse, there appears to be no slackening in the numbers of executions. For example, the notebook of a member of the Security Section in Binh Tan District, Saigon-Gia Dinh Military Region, disclosed that 32 captives were sentenced to death after being held in captivity in that district in the six months between December 1966 and June 1967.[103] Indeed, with the intensification of the campaign of repression that accompanied the launching of the General Offensive in early 1968, the number of executions may well have increased. It may even, in some instances, have got out of hand from the Viet Cong's point of view, for indications of official concern were manifest in a security directive from Trang Bang District, Subregion 1, dated November 20, 1968. While noting that "in the recent past, we have arrested and exterminated more than 100 cruel enemy henchmen who were guilty of many crimes against the people and the Revolution," the directive went on to complain about a "number of major mistakes" committed in the process. It particularly criticized the fact that "we have killed or arrested people without reporting to and requesting directions [from higher echelons], and because of that, receptive civilians or people who did not deserve the death punishment have been wrongly liquidated. . . . "[104]

As the above passage would suggest, the Security Service is acutely aware of the political damage which can result from indiscriminate executions, and it therefore attempts to maintain tight discipline over this activity. Its directives constantly emphasize that executions must be approved by appropriate authorities and "be carried out correctly" and, in particular, that "it is forbidden to execute the accused savagely."[105] Despite these tight strictures, however, a good deal of unauthorized killing seems to take place. The provincial Security Section in I Corps, reporting what is perhaps an extreme example, revealed that out of a total of 198 persons who were killed while in Viet Cong hands from 1964 to 1966, 16 were killed by mistake, another 20 prisoners were killed without orders from higher headquarters, and an unspecified number were killed by the guards who were escorting them to detention camps.[106]

Though the Viet Cong prefer the bullet, some prisoners are executed by stabbing.[107] Many executions take place after a period of detention and interrogation. While some are preceded by a public trial before a People's Court, the great majority are carried out without such formal proceedings. For example, of the 63 persons condemned to death in Ca Mau Province in 1965, only 11 were sentenced by a court in open session.[108] In Rach Gia Province that same year, only five of the 40 persons sentenced to death had been brought to public trial.[109]

In certain cases, the Viet Cong execute prisoners in total secrecy so as to avoid any public knowledge of the action. Such covert executions were mentioned in correspondence dated early 1967 from village and district Security Sections in Thua Thien Province, which reported that several VNQDD Party members had been "secretly liquidated" after interrogation because they were adjudged to "owe a blood debt to the people."[110]

Repression in Contested Areas

If the preceding discussion does not deal in detail with the patterns of repression in the all-important contested areas, the reason for this omission is, simply, that the Viet Cong may, sooner or later, employ all the abovementioned repressive measures in a single contested area, as they tailor their repression to meet the realities of the area's security situation. Thus, when the government's presence in a given village is only marginal, they may be able to operate much as though the village had been "liberated," with in-place reform sessions, home surveillance, and similar measures. On the other hand, at times when the GVN's control is substantial, a local Viet Cong security apparatus may have to limit its activities to assassinations and abductions.

The flexibility of this pattern of operations in the contested areas was spelled out in a Top Secret provincial security directive issued in August 1966:

The situation of disputed areas is very complicated; there is daily struggle between us and the enemy. In some areas we are strong and the enemy is weak, or vice versa. Thus, a disputed area has the characteristics of both liberated and enemy-occupied areas, and security work must be flexible. This means that we must do the maximum of liberated-type activity and also the maximum of occupied-type activity in a way suited to the situation of each different time and place.[111]

The directive went on to state that security organizations in contested areas

... must be half overt and half covert: When the enemy is absent, the overt element will function as in liberated areas, and when the enemy is present, the covert element will function in secret, as in an enemy-occupied area. The organization, duties and working methods of [a] disputed area security apparatus are similar to an occupied township (when the enemy is present). Whenever the area is liberated, the organization duties and working methods used in liberated townships will be introduced.[112]

Because of this ebb-and-flow pattern in the contested areas, and because many Viet Cong districts encompass both GVN-controlled and "liberated" areas, the repressive operations of a provincial or district Security Section often cover a broad spectrum. Some idea of the intensity and breadth of such operations can be garnered from the activity reports that are issued periodically by local Security Sections. For example, a Secret report attributed to an agency of Subregion 1 (which is comparable in size to a province) and dated December 13, 1968, claimed that during the preceding *two months* security personnel from six districts in the Subregion had killed 123 persons, including GVN Psywar, Biet Kich, civil-guard and intelligence personnel, and two Americans; wounded 19 other targets including the Ben Cat District chief; warned 126 persons, and "reeducated" a total of 834 people. As part of the mission of "investigating" the "enemy situation," one district (Cu Chi) had added 16 suspects to its blacklists, another (Trang Bang) had compiled the names of 38 GVN officials and informants, and a third (Ben Cat) had made a roster of 6 suspects and recommended the kidnapping of 25 others.[113]

Another report, also attributed to Subregion 1 but covering security activities for the month following (December 1968), claimed that subordinate districts had killed "43 persons including 15 police, 20 Pacification Team members, 4 intelligence personnel, 1 Regional Force personnel, and 1 Military Security personnel" and had wounded an additional "21 persons—10 police [and] 11 Pacification Team members (one of them the Security Branch chief)." Six persons had been arrested ("5 spies and 1 Police Committee member"), and 55 civilian defense personnel had been "suppressed." The report also claimed that 85 persons had been "reformed" during the month and that some 413 persons had been "educated," including "those who worked for Americans, married Americans, had shady relations, and a passion for gambling."[114] The report, classified "Secret," was dated January 6, 1969.

While reports such as these probably contain some exaggerated claims, particularly with regard to the number of persons assassinated and wounded—figures which the Viet Cong leaders cannot always verify—they do suggest, among other things, the broad scope of a Security Section's activities.

Why Not More?

When one compares the stated intentions of the Viet Cong (as reflected in the large target categories, the number of persons on blacklists, the high quotas assigned to individual units, etc.) with the numbers of persons actually repressed, one may wonder why the Communists do not kill, abduct, and incarcerate more persons than they do. It is clear, for example, that the Viet Cong have not been very successful in eliminating the senior GVN officials, and even at the lower levels, where the targets are comparatively numerous, they do not appear to be achieving anything like the attrition rate which their doctrine requires. Their assaults on the urban areas during the General Offensive in particular, with the probable exception of Hue, seem to have fallen far short of producing the attrition and quotas of victims called for in their security directives.

The fact is, quite simply, that *the Viet Cong want to assassinate or abduct many more people than they are able to*, and their leaders have manifested continual dissatisfaction with the success of repression. Thus, a COSVN security directive of November 1966 complained that

Recent repression work has been crowned with a number of successes but still betrays many shortcomings yet to be overcome. Many areas still displayed a lack of determination when repressing the enemy or fell behind time in their duties, which resulted in failure of their missions. Consequently, a number of requirements of the counterintelligence movement could not be met, such as those for fighting the enemy, consolidating our positions, and countering enemy espionage activities. Prevalent symptoms are: a waivering attitude, lack of determination, [and lack] of courage in the repression mission.[115]

Another COSVN document, in this case a letter addressed in February 1968 to the Saigon-Cholon-Gia Dinh Region Headquarters, stated that the number of enemy "ringleaders killed" during the Tet

Offensive was "still too small," and that "ringleaders of each District or Province administration must be destroyed."[116] A captured activity report dated February 27, 1968, and attributed to the Security Section of the Saigon Region, revealed that local security personnel had "failed to perform missions in accordance with requirements" and that the "number of antirevolutionary personnel exterminated by us was still small."[117] And a similar theme ran through the after-action report of a Communist regiment that had participated in the May offensive against Saigon, which stated that the regiment had "failed to penetrate into the 1st Precinct and failed in its mission of annihilating cruel tyrants."[118]

There is evidence of dissatisfaction with the pace of repression in other towns and cities as well. A provincial security directive captured on March 30, 1968, stated that "urban security agents have not yet fulfilled their tasks" and that "armed reconnaissance [agents] have not yet destroyed or kidnapped cruel and dangerous men"; instead, they "have only destroyed unimportant personnel at villages and hamlets."[119] A Viet Cong circular dated May 16, 1968, and addressed to the Security Sections of districts in Subregion 5 criticized the district personnel for failing to accomplish their assignments during the first ten days of the "Second Offensive Phase." It pointed out that no policeman or important official in the districts' towns or strategic hamlets had been killed, even though many such persons had been sentenced to death (in absentia) by the Party Committee.[120] In numerous other cases, units have been criticized for failure to annihilate tyrants and local GVN administrative persons[121] or to eliminate targeted pacification and intelligence personnel.[122]

Many reasons help to explain why repression often falls short of established goals. By far the most important is the fact that the vast majority of all targets are comparatively well defended. A large proportion either live in towns and cities (which normally are more difficult for the Communists to penetrate) or, if they reside in rural areas, spend their nights in protected outposts. Many targets, such as the Rural Development cadres or National Police personnel, are armed. Thus, if the Viet Cong are to get to most of these targets, they must first suppress the GVN and other Allied forces defending them. One of the principal reasons that repression was not as successful as might have been expected early in the General Offensive was that RVNAF and U.S. forces prevented any sustained Communist control of the urban areas, and many of the Viet Cong's targets in rural parts either went into hiding or fled to the safety of the towns and cities.

In some instances during the Tet Offensive, Communist attacking units did not succeed in penetrating at all. This was true, for instance, in the capital of Quang Tri Province, where local Communist security elements had been directed to concentrate their efforts. The fact that the attacking Communist military units failed to capture their objectives was the reason for the later observation that "nothing had been achieved" by these security forces.[123] Even where Armed Reconnaissance Units or other assassination teams did penetrate the urban areas, the quick reaction of local defensive forces sometimes forced them to abandon their mission. The assassination attempts against President Thieu and General Vien in Saigon, for example, were frustrated because the attacking Viet Cong units were too weak to overcome the police and other GVN security forces defending the residences of these officials.[124]

A number of other reasons helped to account for the Viet Cong's over-all failure to eliminate many of the leaders in Saigon. A postmortem of the Security Service on the Saigon operations during Tet cited a wide variety of shortcomings and errors, ranging from inadequate and inaccurate blacklists to the "hasty assignment of missions":

Generally speaking, the failure of the attempted assassination of the key enemy leaders affects our efforts to smash his organization, command and counterattack, and provides somewhat favorable conditions for him to stabilize the situation, strengthen his force, and motivate the population [to support him]. The reason for this failure stems from a collection of inaccurate information on the addresses of the [key] personalities, the vigilance and careful security measures taken in the protection of these persons, the hasty assignment of missions to our cadres and units in charge, the nonavailability of [military] forces to operate in some areas, the inexperience of the personnel who implemented the plan [security and youth], the shortage of weapons, the delay in the receipt of the orders, the lack of efforts to meet the requirement. . . and lack of determination to fight.[125]

The incidence of repression is further limited by various other kinds of GVN and Allied counteroperations, such as the arrest by Saigon police of some 516 Viet Cong agents and demolition experts in the capital during the last three months of 1968.[126]

Sometimes, local security forces are too poorly organized or simply too weak to carry out their missions. This is confirmed, for example, by the following account in an activity report of October 13, 1968, prepared by a security agency in Gia Lai Province:

In the district seat and province capital the mission of annihilating the cruel tyrants and reactionaries was not carried out fully, and the legal reconnaissance and armed forces were not built up. As a result, we failed to kill important ringleaders and frighten their henchmen.

The mission of building up hamlet and village security cadres and the secret security network and agencies in the newly-liberated areas was not properly carried out, and the legal position [in the temporarily enemy-controlled areas] was weak. Therefore, we could not fully know the situation. This prevented us from resolutely coping with the enemy spies and oppressing the reactionaries.[127]

At other times, failure to complete a mission may be due to a combination of factors, not the least of which are the precautionary measures frequently taken by GVN targets. Consider, for example, this passage from a training document produced by the Binh Tan Propaganda and Training Section in 1967:

Breaking the enemy's control machinery and killing tyrants:
This task has not been satisfactorily accomplished, since we did not have enough personnel in the area. Another reason was that the tyrants, those deserving the name, were well aware of the peril to their lives and went into perfect hiding. Some of them were followed for eight long months without our being able to kill them. When our personnel were available, the conditions were unfavorable, and when they were seen alone, we had no personnel available. One of them was followed on his way home from the office. We intended to shoot him at his door, but he immediately locked it as soon as he entered the house. Pulling out our guns, we knocked on the door. He shouted to us for the password. We played honest citizens by insisting: "By the heavens! We are all natives of this place! Why do you ask us for the password?"

"Well, let's see!" he said, swiftly turning back to snatch his pistol from a coat hung on a peg. We outshot him, killing him.

We therefore concluded that we can kill the tyrants with an adequate force at our disposal. Otherwise, the mission requires time, surveillance and cost. An on-the-spot force would fit perfectly.[128]

Occasionally, a mission fails because reconnaissance units have been inadequately armed or grossly mismanaged. One such instance is described as follows in a critique of the Go Dau District Security Section, Tay Ninh Province, prepared by a senior cadre of Tay Ninh's provincial Security Section:

The employment of [the] Armed Reconnaissance Unit was not successful. It was not used properly for the armed reconnaissance mission of the security branch, but it was assigned miscellaneous missions such as providing security observers along routes, supervising civilian laborers, conducting propaganda and fund drives, performing transportation activities, etc. . . . In the meantime, the missions of killing and breaking the oppressive control of the tyrants were not carried out. There was no specific objective for each activity and the soldiers in the unit did not discuss the plan. Though they were successively assigned to weak areas, their success was meager. In addition, they were not thoroughly indoctrinated and, as a result of this, they were often envious' and competed with each other. Even in the leadership, there were certain problems in some cases. In short, the Armed Reconnaissance Unit was not used properly for the appropriate mission. So the results were limited. . . .

The equipment of the Armed Reconnaissance Unit was poor. It had no modern weapons except for an inadequate number of K53 and CKC [carbines]. In some cases, the Party Chapters discovered the tyrants and had the opportunity to kill them, but they did not contact the Armed Reconnaissance Unit, because the latter did not have modern weapons; they had to contact other forces which had modern weapons.[129]

"Low determination" is frequently cited in Communist reports as one of the principal reasons for not achieving better results. An August 1968 report, believed to have been written by a cadre in the 7th Precinct of Saigon, stated that "a number of objectives concerning the killing of tyrants and the breaking of the enemy's oppressive control were attempted but were not successfully accomplished because of [the comrades'] low determination." The cadre went on to say that "after reviewing the activities, additional plans were drafted and erroneous thoughts corrected." But the author obviously still had some doubts, for he added: "Some agents made many promises, but I must wait for the results. . . ."[130] In at least one case, "low determination" stemmed from the fear of local Viet Cong cadres that their relatives would be killed: In a notebook containing entries from April 1967 to May 1968, a cadre of Ba To District, Quang Ngai Province, revealed that the elimination of GVN administrative personnel had not been successful in some areas of the district because many of the Viet Cong village cadres were related to the GVN targets selected for liquidation and did not want to have their relatives assassinated.[131]

5 The Alternative to Repression

In the preceding discussion of the purposes of repression, brief mention was made of the role which repression plays in facilitating Communist proselytizing efforts among the GVN's civilian and military bureaucracies. Since, under certain circumstances, this facet of Communist operations could prove critical to the future cohesion and stability of the GVN, a more detailed examination of the interrelationship between repression and proselytizing would seem warranted.

Proselytizing

First, a few comments about Viet Cong proselytizing in general. In the course of the past few years, the Viet Cong have put increasing emphasis on recruiting persons from all levels of the GVN's military and civilian bureaucracies to the side of the Revolution. As the third prong of the Communists' fundamental strategy of the "three-pronged attack," military proselytizing, for example, has been placed on an equal status with the other military and political activities which constitute the first two prongs of this strategic triad. Considerable human resources have been committed to the effort, and proselytizing has received major organizational recognition in the "Military and Civilian Proselytizing Sections" which the Viet Cong have established as integral components of their provincial, district, and village structures. At the province level, for example, one usually finds a Military Proselytizing Section and a separate Civilian Proselytizing Section attached to the Province Party Committee, and additional Military and Civilian Proselytizing elements will be attached to the Political Staff of the provincial military headquarters.

Proselytizing campaigns employ a variety of media, including formal entertainment groups that travel from village to village; clandestine newspapers and radio transmitters; and numerous posters, leaflets, and other printed matter. A good deal of effort is concentrated on "face-to-face" indoctrination by propaganda cadres at the village markets, by secret propagandists who have been planted within government ranks, and by local cadres making house-to-house visits at the hamlet level. The Viet Cong seem to consider the relatives of persons serving in the GVN their most effective vehicles, and GVN-connected families living in VC-controlled or contested areas are constantly pressured to write to or visit their sons, brothers, or husbands in order to persuade them to defect and join forces with the Revolution.

The campaigns are differentated according to individual target groups (officers are approached differently from enlisted men, intellectuals from urban workers, etc.), and they often are tailored to specific local grievances they seek to exploit. But they all place heavy emphasis on appeals to "nationalism," "anticolonialism," and "anti-Americanism," the central theme being that the National Liberation Front is fighting a "just war" against the American imperialists and their Vietnamese lackeys, that the forces of this Revolution are gaining strength day by day and will prove victorious in the end, and that to assist in this great patriotic struggle is the sacred duty of all the Vietnamese, including the misguided who have thoughtlessly sided with, or have been "duped" into joining, the GVN.

The Carrot and the Stick

Even though much of this proselytizing would appear, on the surface, to lean heavily on positive appeals to "patriotism" and "nationalism," these efforts at persuasion are nearly always under-lined by a manifest capability and proven willingness to use physical coercion if need be. This is particularly true in the case of those government officials, military officers, and other target categories which the Viet Cong have marked down for repression. For in proselytizing among them, the Viet Cong frequently offer these targets the stark choice of either continuing in the service of the GVN and risking certain repression, or joining forces with the Revolution and earning the clemency and perhaps even the favor of the Communists. To those who opt for accommodation, the Viet Cong offer either to mitigate or to erase altogether any punishment due for past crimes. To persons who provide particularly important and meritorious services to the Revolution, they hold out the possibility of rewarding positions and advancement within their ranks. In other words, the proffer of clemency is the carrot that accompanies the stick of repression.

The essence of this "carrot-and-stick" approach is reflected in the maxims of the Security Service that "repression [must be] carefully coordinated with clemency" and "punishment closely coordinated with reform." A high-level security directive has summed up the "spirit and content" of this policy in the context of repressing "spies and reactionaries" as:

Strictly punish instigators, tyrants, and other elements who oppose us.
Tolerate those who will repent or those who are bribed or forced [to assist the enemy].
Decrease or forgive the crimes of those who acquire merits and, at the same time, reward the people who gain outstanding achievements. [1]

Several characteristics of this policy of clemency-and-reform deserve comment. In the first place, the Viet Cong make a distinction between persons who are only marginally aligned with the GVN (having been "bribed" or "forced" into working for the government) and those who have knowingly volunteered their services or prove strongly committed to the government side. As the foregoing quotation suggests, the former as a rule are treated with considerably more leniency than the latter. Second, the Viet Cong are inclined to "tolerate," and not repress, those minor offenders who "faithfully repent" their past associations with the GVN. In Viet Cong usage, a person normally is expected to demonstrate his repentance by the complete cessation of all unauthorized association with the GVN (by resignation or desertion), a written confession of and apology for all past "crimes," and a formal promise never to return to the service of the government. He must also prove willing to accept the indoctrination and "reform" of the Communists and must be ready to abide by "all policies laid down by the Party."[2] In other words, he must be ready to come to a disciplined heel.

Third, of persons who are judged to have committed serious offenses against the Revolution and who are classified as "major" tyrants or reactionaries, more is required if repression is to be avoided or even mitigated. They not only must "repent" but must also "atone" for their past crimes through some positive and demonstrable service to the Revolution. Atonement (which the Viet Cong term "acquiring merits") takes varying forms, including such activities as providing intelligence, acting as fifth-columnist or propagandist for the Front, assassinating other tyrants, and actually bearing arms in a Viet Cong unit. Generally speaking, the greater the target's crime, the greater the service required if he is to receive absolution.

Finally, for those who provide exceptional service to the movement and show "outstanding achievements," there is the promise of reward. Although enemy documents are somewhat vague as to the precise nature of the rewards, these apparently include Liberation Front medals and commendations, opportunities for service and advancement within the Viet Cong structure (even the possibility of Party membership), and "responsible positions" in the administration which the Communists expect to establish in the South once the liberation has been consummated.[3]

The obvious objective of this policy is to erode the cohesion and morale of the opponent; it is the Communist counterpart of the GVN's Chieu Hoi program. Through it, the Viet Cong seek to induce desertions and defections from the government's ranks, to encourage passivity among GVN military and civilian officials (by offering to "record the merits" of those who refrain from carrying out the orders of their superiors), and to build up subversive and intelligence networks within the government bureaucracies. By forcing former GVN officials to publicly recant all past activities and associations—a gesture to which they appear to attach considerable propaganda value—the Viet Cong aim to gain prestige for their movement and denigrate the government in the eyes of the local population. Another aim is to sow suspicion within the ranks of the GVN. By making it known that government officials will be spared or rewarded if they agree to become "in-place" agents of the Viet Cong, the Communists hope to undermine cohesion within the government, as officials become uncertain about the extent to which they may trust their colleagues.[4]

There is also a solid rationale for the practice of requiring some kind of positive service from those who would seek absolution. In the first place, it preserves and fortifies the Viet Cong's fundamental moral doctrine that "penance" must be done for past crimes and that any remission of punishment must be adequately justified. Secondly, and viewed more pragmatically, the Viet Cong can be relatively certain of the sincerity of the defector who is willing to back his words with positive deeds. As a general rule, they tend to regard the would-be turncoat with considerable suspicion, fearing that he may be a government plant or that his change of heart is only a matter of immediate convenience.[5] The requirement for some positive action in the service of the Revolution thus becomes a useful test of an individual's sincerity and long-run intentions. It is also a way of committing irrevocably any opportunists who might otherwise be inclined to shift back to the GVN at a later date. Since the types of service usually required by the Communists (spying, assassination, fifth-column activity, etc.) are traitorous and carry severe penalties if uncovered by the GVN, the one who performs such services becomes, in effect, hostage to the Viet Cong; he may go back to the government only at the peril of being denounced by his former Communist mentors. Finally, and most important, those former GVN persons who can be induced to perform such service are highly useful to the Communists as invaluable sources of intelligence, covert political action, and at times even combat support.

Warnings and Other Communication Media

In communicating to targets the options that are open to them, the Communists employ both general propaganda appeals outlining the Front's "policy of leniency" (which are disseminated through leaflets, propaganda meetings in the villages, radio broadcasts, Front newspapers, and the like) and personalized warnings to specific targets (usually sent in the form of messages through relatives or in letters). While both the carrot and the stick usually are evident, the personalized forms of communication depend most heavily on naked threats.

The general appeals mostly echo the policy statements concerning the treatment of former government personnel which are set down in the National Liberation Front program issued in August 1967. This program, while firmly warning that "the diehard cruel agents of the U.S. imperialists" would be "severely punished," gave prominence to the Front's policies of "leniency" and "reward" for those "puppet officers and men" and "puppet officials" who returned to the "just cause." It even differentiated among the kinds of treatment that various individuals might expect to receive, depending on their contributions to the Revolution. Thus, persons from the "puppet army and administration" who rendered services to the Front would be "rewarded and entrusted with responsible jobs." Individuals who "sympathize with and support the struggle" or "refuse to carry out orders of the U.S. and puppets to harm the people" would "have their merits recorded." A "welcome" and "equal treatment" were proffered to individuals or units who defect from "the puppet army and voluntarily apply to join" the Front, and captured officers and men were assured "humanitarian treatment and clemency." "Equal treatment" was also promised to "those functionaries of the puppet administration who volunteer to serve the country and the people in the state machine after the liberation of South Vietnam." A pardon awaited "those in the puppet army and the puppet administration at any level who have committed crimes against the people but are now sincerely repentant." Finally, the program pledged, "those who redeem their crimes by meritorious deeds will be rewarded accordingly."[6]

The above policies have received considerable prominence in Viet Cong propaganda campaigns throughout the South.[7] They appeared, in condensed form, in the "Nine-Point Policies Regarding the Newly Liberated Cities," which the Communists distributed in many urban areas at the time of the 1968 Tet Offensive. Points V and VI of this widely disseminated policy statement read:

V. GVN personnel and those working for the US imperialists and their henchmen will be welcomed if they wish to serve the Revolutionary Government.

However, they must absolutely obey the orders of the Revolutionary Government and carry out its policies and they must hand over the property and files of their organizations.

VI. Puppet officers and soldiers who [have] achieved merit against the Americans in favor of the Nation will be recompensed. Those who [have been] judged guilty by the people but now feel sincerely apologetic for what they have done will be given clemency. Those who want to return home will be given permission to do so.[8]

However, other policy pronouncements issued during Tet balanced these inducements with warnings about the firm treatment awaiting those who refused to cooperate with Communist forces. Article 5 of an "Order" issued by the Revolutionary Council of the Anti-Thieu/Ky Civilian and Military United Forces of Khanh Hoa Province is one example:

Those who continue to display their faithfulness to Thieu/Ky and stubbornly persist in acting against the Anti-Thieu/Ky Civilian and Military United Forces will be arrested and sentenced by the Revolutionary Council in accordance with its previously published policy based on the opinion of the people. Those who violate the freedom and democracy of the people of all walks of life will be severely punished. Delinquent persons caught in the act will be arrested and sent to the Revolutionary Council . . . .[9]

One of the most recent Communist policy statements concerning the treatment to be given to GVN persons who "cross over to the side" of the Revolution was contained in the "12-Point Program" issued by the "Provisional Revolutionary Government of the Republic of South Vietnam" in June 1969. Point 9 of this action program promised:

To encourage, welcome, and properly reward those officers and men of the puppet army and police and those functionaries of the puppet administration who cross over to the side of the people after accomplishing meritorious deeds. To grant special encouragement and rewards to those puppet army and police units that cross over to the side of the Provisional Revolutionary Government.

To show leniency [to], and refrain from any discrimination against, those guilty persons who repent and truly rejoin the ranks of the people . . . .[10]

Complementing these more general, public appeals are the personalized warnings to individual targets. Although their content varies from case to case, they usually place the target on notice that his "crimes" have come to the Viet Cong's attention and that, unless he resigns his position, defects, or otherwise accommodates himself to the Front to "atone" for these crimes, he will be killed or punished.

In transmitting these warnings, the Viet Cong make extensive use of any accessible relatives or dependents of persons serving in the GVN. One proselytizing directive, emphasizing this channel, urged all cadres to "talk openly to the dependents so they will tell their husbands, sons, or brothers to return [to the ranks of the Viet Cong] and gain achievements in order to [atone for] their former crimes."[11] Relatives seem to be favored by the Viet Cong because they provide direct and credible channels to the targets. To the individual target who is approached through members of his family, this very fact implies convincingly that the relatives used in the transmission belt may be hostages to his own good behavior. Indeed, Viet Cong proselytizers often stress the welfare of the target's family as an important consideration in his choice of action. Thus, typically, the surrender leaflet used during the occupation of Hue warned ARVN troops who continued to hide out in that city that "to remain hidden means you want to oppose the people. Not only will you bring disaster upon yourselves, you also jeopardize the lives of your families, your wives and children . . . ."[12] In some instances, even more specific threats of reprisals against relatives are employed.[13]

The mails are another widely-used channel for personalized warnings—usually addressed to the target at his home. The aforementioned security directive issued by Region II described the mission of warning by mail:

As far as the elimination of traitors and tyrants is concerned, we have to carry out the mission of warning the guilty elements who have not yet been exterminated. We will frighten them and make them stop their activities and reduce their sabotage against the Revolution. We will push them to secretly give in to our side . . . .

We will mail warning letters to the counterrevolutionary elements . . . warn them one by one . . . we will encourage them to give in. We can force them from higher to lower echelon, to show their repentance.[14]

Another document, dated December 1968 and attributed to a District Party Committee of Ca Mau Province, explained how such warning letters should be tailored to individual targets. In military proselytizing activities, "many letters" were to be written to enemy soldiers and officers to impel them to "return to the Revolution." Then:

To succeed in motivating them, we must know the record of each of them, make a list of their names and crimes. Tell each of them about the crimes he has committed and inform him that should he not repent for his crimes, he will be punished by the people or even by his own sisters or brothers.[15]

Sometimes, warnings are addressed to several targets at one time in the form of "Public Denunciations." One of these, issued in the name of the National Liberation Front Committee of Tan An District on May 14, 1968, accused eight local GVN officials of "antirevolutionary activities" and warned them that death would ensue if they did not resign from their positions and redeem themselves.[16]

Individual targets may receive several warnings before action is taken against them. Indeed, a policy directive concerning the repression of VNQDD Party members stipulated that VNQDD Village Committee members were to be "eliminated" if they "continue to sabotage the Revolution, after they have been indoctrinated *and have been warned several times . . . .* "(Emphasis added)[17]

The evidence from captured documents would tend to suggest that personalized warnings are a common phenomenon in the South, and that for every GVN official or employee assassinated or kidnapped several others may be warned. This inference is supported in part by activity reports of the Security Service which list the number of warnings delivered by particular agencies in a given time. To cite a few examples of many, a District Committee in Ba Bien Province reported eliminating 4 GVN administrative officials and warning 13 others during the month of June 1968; the Security Service of a second Viet Cong district (Lai Thieu) claimed to have killed 3 local administrative officials and warned 8 others during the first six weeks of 1968; and a third district (Duyen Hai, Subregion 4) reported killing 10 persons and warning 174 others (133 "by letter") between January 31 and March 15, 1968.[18] This coupling of warnings with assassinations, which is quite common in Viet Cong reporting, reflects the close link between these activities. Assassinations, of course, enhance the credibility of the warnings.

The intimate connection between warnings and actual repression in Viet Cong operations is perhaps best summed up in an October 1968 provincial directive concerning the "task of killing wicked tyrants and eliminating traitors, and the task of launching political attacks" during the General Offensive:

To make the people in towns and cities [and the] puppet soldiers dare rise up and follow the Revolution, the important thing is that we must boldly and resolutely kill wicked tyrants and eliminate traitors. This action must be carried out concurrently with a strong and continuous political attack aimed at puppet troops, puppet government, public security and police personnel, spies and secret agents, reactionary elements, and stubborn wicked tyrants. We must resort to resolute measures and actions to suppress the enemy's morale.[19]

The directive went on to specify how this "political attack" was to be conducted and how the threat of repression was to be employed to impel tyrants to come to terms with the Viet Cong. It particularly emphasized the importance of conveying to the targets that there was a "way out of their plight" through accommodation and atonement, and pointed out that it was "not advisable to drive them into a dead-end alley" which would only make them "all the more reckless and rash":

During the political attack, *we must cite the cases of former wicked tyrants who mended their ways by achieving merits to atone for their crimes; not only will they benefit by our clemency, but their merits may also be considered for commendation or award.* At the same time, we shall severely punish those stubborn wicked tyrants who do not mend their ways and who refuse to surrender themselves to the Revolution.

Through the task of investigating the crimes of stubborn wicked tyrants, we must work out plans to kill them immediately. *As for those whom we have not been able to kill, we must use leaflets, slogans, banners, private letters, indictments, and warning letters to arouse public opinion, to denounce them to the people, to directly tell their families that if they do not mend their ways, surrender themselves and achieve merits to atone for their crimes, they will be punished.* (These measures must be applied regularly. Especially, letters of warning must be sent many times, with [our agents] following up any change [in the tyrants' attitude]. The . . . letters must mention the new crimes which we have come to know of.) *Attention must be paid to showing them a way out of their plight. It is not advisable to drive them into a dead-end alley [where] they will become all the more reckless and rash.* This political attack is also applicable to stubborn wicked tyrants in the ranks of puppet troops.[20]

"Puppet soldiers" were to be motivated to kill Americans and "wicked tyrants" as a means of achieving "merits" and as a way to help "save themselves and their families":

Concurrently with conducting propaganda to enlighten puppet soldiers polit-ically, we must strongly motivate them to turn their weapons back to kill their commanders and the Americans. We may use . . . slogans like: "[You] must resolutely turn your weapon back to kill the Americans and stubborn wicked tyrants in order to save yourselves, to achieve merit in favor of the Revolution" or (while in combat) "lay down your arms to let the Liberation Troops kill the stubborn wicked tyrants." By many forms [of propaganda] and with many appropriate slogans, *we must somehow show them that to turn their weapons back to kill the Americans and their wicked and stubborn [RVNAF] Unit Commanders any time they can, to avoid killing the people and to seek ways to return to the people, are patriotic acts helping them to save themselves and their families and to achieve merits in favor of the Revolution.* When killing wicked tyrants and eliminating traitors, with our aim directed at the wicked ringleaders, we must make propaganda to increase the scope of our victories, arouse enthusiasm among cadres, soldiers and the people, and incite the people to rise to perform revolutionary actions with a firm standpoint, thus lowering the prestige of the enemy.[21]

"Carrot and Stick" in Operation

The captured documents provide numerous illustrations of how the carrot-and-stick principle governs Communist operations in the South. It is evident, for example, in the policies which the Communists laid down for the handling of GVN prisoners during the Tet Offensive. According to the MACV summary of a Top Secret proselytizing directive issued by the Political Department of Military Region V on November 10, 1967, the disposition of government prisoners during the General Offensive and Uprising in the cities and towns was to be as follows:

— Tyrants and religious officials were to be prosecuted by security cadres.

— Troops captured in combat and those who refused to report to Viet Cong authorities (after an area was occupied) were to be sent to thought-reform camps.

— Defectors were to be indoctrinated and then released on the spot.

— Individual officers or enlisted men who had "scored credits" before siding with the Revolution were to be welcomed and recommended for awards. However, the directive cautioned that such persons should not be "overpraised" and that even in these cases, their past crimes were to be pointed out to them.

— An enemy unit which staged a military revolt was to be welcomed by a meeting, kept intact, and assigned to Viet Cong provincial units.

— No military attacks were to be directed against any government unit which declared itself as "dissident" from the RVNAF or "neutral." [22]

Carrot and stick are also apparent in the guidelines which the Viet Cong set down for the repression of specific target groups. Consider, for example, a March 1968 security directive which outlined the policies to be followed in the repression of VNQDD officials and members. While urging that an all-out effort be made to "strongly and constantly repress" followers of that party, the directive specifically exempted two categories of persons from severe punishment. First, "those who were subject to elimination, but have shown their regrets by sending letters to us expressing their intention to surrender and atone for their faults ... will not be sentenced to death." Second, VNQDD members belonging to "the poor and middle farmers' class who have recently joined [the VNQDD] because of lies or ignorance and now want to defect may be tolerated and indoctrinated." The latter group, however, as a test of their good faith, were to "work for the village [apparatus] and show that they are innocent." Then "if it is found that they can improve themselves, we may leave them in [the] local areas for further indoctrination under the sponsorship of their families." [23]

The carrot-and-stick principle is also apparent in the manner in which Viet Cong security cadres present the alternatives open to local GVN officials and administrative personnel. In many cases, these targets are given the stark choice of either cooperating with the Viet Cong or facing execution. A directive issued in May 1967 to Viet Cong village agencies in Chau Duc District is indicative of this "either-or" approach: As part of the over-all mission of "disrupting" the newly-elected GVN village and hamlet administrative apparatus in that district, local Communist cadres were to conduct an investigation by which to sift out those newly-elected officials who were likely to be receptive to Viet Cong proselytizing from those who would appear to be "recalcitrant." The former were to be allowed to retain their positions so that they might secretly work for the Viet Cong; those who proved recalcitrant, on the other hand, were to be eliminated.[24] Other documents also refer to this policy of assassinating GVN officials who display an uncooperative attitude toward local Viet Cong cadres.[25]

One example of an "either-or" type of personal warning to a local official is provided in a captured letter, dated December 12, 1969, addressed to a hamlet chief in Binh Dinh Province. In this letter, the hamlet chief was promised clemency from the Revolution if he cooperated with local Viet Cong cadres and put an end to his "cruel" activities. If he refused, the warning stated that he would be executed by the Viet Cong as soon as the Communist forces had defeated the RVNAF or within twenty-four hours after a total American troop withdrawal from Vietnam.[26]

A 1967 provincial directive which set down guidelines for the repression of administrative personnel at the village and hamlet level suggested several alternative methods of handling any GVN officials who might wish an accommodation with the Viet Cong. It emphasized that "repression work should be performed in agreement with the three-pronged tactic" and "should serve the political purposes of the local areas." In the process of repression,

. . . if any local [RVN] administrative personnel want, out of fear, to meet us to confess their crimes, we can use either of the following methods:

If he is a hamlet official, having the capability of doing some useful work elsewhere, then we will find a means to transfer him to that place, where *he will be told to achieve something to atone for his faults.* If not, we will prevent him from carrying on his present work. If he is a village administrative personnel, we also have to use the above means. But if he does not have the capability of performing any other missions in another place, while being in a sensitive village, where our mission is to cut down all of its administrative personnel, then we *must force him to resign or make him accomplish a number of tasks for us during a certain period of time, or get him to kill another village official to make up for his faults.* [27]

Encouraging would-be defectors to kill their former colleagues or superiors as a way of demonstrating their sincerity and atoning for past crimes is by no means uncommon. A May 1969 security directive attributed to the Can Duoc District Unit, Subregion 3, contained a specific reference to this means of "gaining merits":

Some tyrants, who are being threatened, want to atone for their crimes by gaining merits. This depends on the specific circumstances of each tyrant. We can appeal to them to cooperate with us and employ them in the service of exterminating [other] wicked tyrants and to help break the enemy's hold on the area. [28]

This practice was evident also in a letter addressed to a member of an RVNAF reconnaissance unit warning the addressee that his district was to be liberated in the very near future and that, to save his life, he would have to defect and bring weapons to the Viet Cong or to act against the "puppet army" by killing tyrants.[29] Or, consider a February 1968 report attributed to the Political Staff of the Quang Da Special Zone, Military Region V, which disclosed that during a Viet Cong attack on a GVN post a number of RVNAF enlisted men surrendered and volunteered to fight against their former comrades-in-arms. The Viet Cong unit accepted their offer *after having them kill those they assumed loyal to the RVNAF.* The defectors then fought side by side with the Viet Cong for a whole day. When the Communist forces withdrew, however, they did not take the defectors with them, but encouraged them to return to their units and continue to serve the Viet Cong cause from within the RVNAF.[30]

Among instances in which GVN personnel either planned to or did kill "tyrants" before defecting is one reported by the Security Section of Cu Chi District, where, as a result of local proselytizing efforts, three government soldiers had decided to defect, but before their defection were planning to "suppress tyrants" to make up for their own past mistakes.[31] The Personal History Statements that record the background of persons serving in Viet Cong units also provide instances of former GVN followers who claim to have assassinated one or more of their colleagues prior to joining the Communists.[32]

Aside from administering punishments directly to his former allies or associates, a target may "gain merits" and "atone" for past crimes by assisting the Viet Cong in identifying or hunting down "tyrants." Presumably, Communist cadres were more than willing to "record the merits" of the company executive officer of the National Police Field Forces who helped the Viet Cong track down GVN officials during the occupation of Hue,[33] or of the six GVN officials who denounced four of their colleagues to security cadres in My Phong Village.[34]

On occasion, the Viet Cong may require a financial contribution from their targets, as in the case of the policeman from Bien Hoa Province who received an extortion letter demanding money in return for the "clemency" which the Viet Cong had granted him.[35] Targets may also gain merits by turning in weapons or other equipment to the Viet Cong, and by providing them with classified government documents.[36]

One of the more common forms of atonement exacted by the Communists is fifth-column activity. Here again, targets frequently are approached through their families. One proselytizing directive, for example, urged local cadres to convince the families of GVN servicemen that it was a crime for these soldiers to remain loyal to the government, and that they as wives, parents, and relatives should persuade the GVN servicemen "to operate for the Revolution as fifth-columnists in the enemy ranks in order to serve their families and the Fatherland."[37]

The Viet Cong make strenuous efforts to recruit fifth-columnists and "sympathizers" from all levels of the GVN's civilian and military bureaucracies. Some are enlisted "in place" (having been covertly approached by Viet Cong agents, or by relatives, or through the mails), while many others (including large numbers of military fifth-columnists) are recruited after capture or desertion and are reintroduced into their units following a period of indoctrination and training.

Fifth-columnists may be called upon to carry out a variety of missions for their Communist case officers. According to a planning document of 1967:

The fifth-columnists must be trained and used very carefully. They can be used to provide information to us or to motivate the puppet soldiers to claim their privileges [or] refuse to go on sweep or search operations; [they can] support the struggle of the masses against the [GVN's] control system and acts of terrorism . . .; [they can] secretly eliminate the tyrants and . . . help us seize the weapons of the enemy; or [they can] support and participate in the uprising of the people to break the enemy control when the uprising takes place. [38]

From the data at hand, it is not possible to assess with any confidence the extent to which such proselytizing efforts have succeeded in causing erosion and subversion in the GVN structure; given the frequent mention of fifth-column activities in captured documents and the Communists' apparent success in penetrating the government for the acquisition of intelligence, one may assume that the carrot-and-stick policy has had some effect. What is quite clear, however, is that the Viet Cong perceive this policy as potentially effective in hastening the disintegration of the GVN and, therefore, are investing substantial time and effort in it.

6 Some Implications for the Future

GVN Perceptions

As has been shown, the targets of Viet Cong repression include leadership elements from all echelons of the GVN's administrative hierarchy, from such low-level personnel as hamlet and city-ward chiefs to the senior officials in Saigon. Also among the target groups are the civilian and military figures who now control the government's major instruments of power: ARVN and other military officers, officials of the National Police, and personnel commanding the several investigatory and security agencies. There is every reason to assume that members of all these target groups have very pessimistic expectations as to their ultimate fate should a Communist regime come to power in South Vietnam.

Above all, they must be fully aware that they constitute the chief targets for the Communist campaign of repression. They see the captured blacklists containing the names of those marked for execution and read the constant flow of intercepted enemy directives urging the liquidation of all government "tyrants" and "reactionaries." Many have no doubt been recipients of Viet Cong "warnings," and many more probably know of immediate colleagues who have been assassinated or abducted. They also know that during the 25-day occupation of Hue—the one city which the Communists were able to hold for any length of time during the Tet Offensive—the extermination of officials and other government-connected persons was systematic and brutal.

Large numbers of civilian and military officials must be aware that at one time or another they have perpetrated acts that constitute "serious crimes" by the standards of the Viet Cong and as a result have very likely been listed among those who owe a "blood debt" to the Revolution. Indeed, some GVN officials probably know themselves to be multiple offenders in Communist eyes. One need only imagine, for example, the probable expectations of a Catholic ARVN officer, a refugee from North Vietnam, who is a member of the Dai Viet Party and whose major career assignments have been with the Military Security Service.

Perceptions based on the more recent experience of Communist repression are reinforced by the knowledge of what happened in

North Vietnam during the 1953-1956 Land Reform campaign, when many tens of thousands of "landlords," "traitors," and "reactionaries" were put to death or sent to forced-labor camps. The campaign has been described in the open literature, and there is no need here to recount the bloody story.[1] It is worth noting, however, that, even though the Land Reform was in many ways unique, there are interesting parallels between some of the practices followed during that campaign and the pattern of repression in the South today. They include the preparation of blacklists to designate those who are to be eliminated, the classification of the population by different letters of the alphabet as a guideline for the appropriate degree of repression, the public denunciation sessions where victims were required to confess their alleged crimes before their fellow-villagers, the use of People's Tribunals to pass sentence, and the setting of quotas for the number of persons to be killed in each village.[2] These quotas varied in the course of the Land Reform campaign: At one point, it was set at from three to five per village; during a later stage, "the number of death sentences was fixed at a minimum of five per village."[3]

During the public denunciation sessions, the "landlords"—many of whom possessed little more land than their fellow-villagers—were time and again accused of the most heinous crimes and "blood debts" (rape, torture, the slaughter of innocent children, counter-revolutionary activities, etc.), which generally had no basis in fact. If the victims of these accusations proved recalcitrant—that is, if they persisted in affirming their innocence—they often were shot. If, on the other hand, they assumed a repentant stance and meekly confessed to all crimes, their "punishment was likely to be less severe."[4] Throughout these denunciation sessions, and in the course of the Land Reform campaign as a whole, local Party propagandists made a concerted effort to animate the people to a condition of "mass anger," to instill in them a deep hatred of the targets of the campaign, and to motivate the peasants to participate fully in the denunciation and execution of the landlords. Commenting on this aspect of the campaign, one author has observed:

In forcing them to denounce and kill landlords, the party wanted to make the peasants share in the blood-guilt. Thus, those who had directly or indirectly participated in the massacre, being morally and politically compromised, were forced to side with the party through fear of retaliation.[5]

It seems likely that similar considerations underlie the Viet Cong's current campaign to foment hatred of the GVN and to persuade local populations to participate in the extermination of "tyrants" and "reactionaries."

Although the central purpose of the Land Reform campaign was "the liquidation of the landowning class and the subsequent establishment of a proletarian dictatorship in the countryside," including, of course, collectivization of the land,[6] there is strong reason to believe that the campaign was also used as a convenient pretext for purging the North of potential oppositionists and for reprisals against those who had worked for or were suspected of having cooperated with the French.[7] Charges of "spying" and other "traitorous" behavior designed to "sabotage the Revolution" were common, although frequently, like many other charges, they had little or no basis in fact. According to one account:

Even those who had served the DRV administration and had been decorated by Ho Chi Minh for their achievements were charged with deliberately penetrating the administrative and political structure of the country in order to sabotage the Revolution. No proof was required, and it was sufficient evidence for someone to have seen a landlord waving at a French aircraft, for instance, to condemn him as a spy working for the enemy.[8]

Estimates vary as to the total number of persons who were killed or sent to concentration camps during this campaign. According to Joseph Buttinger, "it is generally believed that the number killed was between 10,000 and 15,000 and that between 50,000 and 100,000 were deported and imprisoned."[9] Bernard Fall, writing in 1963, reported as "the best educated guesses" that "probably close to 50,000 North Vietnamese were executed in connection with the land reform and . . . at least twice as many were arrested and sent to forced labor camps."[10] A much higher figure was suggested by P.J. Honey, who wrote that "hundreds of thousands of patently guiltless people were done to death in the most cruel fashion" during the campaign.[11] The Frenchman Gérard Tongas, a university professor who remained in the North until 1959, claimed that the "indescribable butchery resulted in one hundred thousand deaths."[12]

Hoang Van Chi, in his detailed study of the Land Reform campaign, estimates that "half a million Vietnamese (4 per cent of the population of North Vietnam) were sacrificed" during that campaign.[13] He cites refugee reports to the effect that "the whole countryside of North Vietnam was white with the turbans of mourners" and estimates that "as many" people died in concentration camps or from suicide brought on by the Land Reform campaign as were publicly executed. He goes on to state that even "a far greater number of landlords' famililies—the majority of these being small children— died from starvation" as a direct result of the economic and social "isolation" policies instituted during the campaign.[14] According to Chi, "the staggering size of the death toll could not have surprised the Vietnamese Communists, for their maxim during the days of terror was 'It is better to kill ten innocent people than to let one enemy escape'."[15]

While the precise number of those who perished or were imprisoned will probably never be known, there can be little doubt that it was very large. Nor can there be any doubt that it would have been even greater had it not been for the fact that many thousands of potential victims (including both staunchly anti-Communist Catholics and large numbers of Vietnamese military and civilian personnel who had served under the French) escaped to South Vietnam during the 300-day "freedom of movement" period provided for in the Geneva Agreements.

The bloody record of the Land Reform campaign is well remembered by many GVN persons in the South today; it was widely publicized during the Diem regime, and there are, of course, many Northerners in the present ranks of GVN officials. Furthermore, government officials, military officers, and cadres must be aware that many of the victims of the Land Reform committed far less severe "crimes" against the Communists than those who are being targeted for elimination in the South today.

The net effect of this knowledge, combined with the more recent experience, is to convince many GVN civilian and military officials that they would become the victims of a major bloodbath if the Communists were to assume power. This is not to say that such a bloodbath is certain to occur in the event of a Communist rise to power. But it is clear that many in the South would expect one. They would, of course, also expect other punitive measures, such as the confiscation of their land holdings and other property. (The confiscation of "land owned by traitors and wicked tyrants" is already a common practice in Viet Cong-controlled areas.)[16]

One very pessimistic forecast was provided by former Prime Minister Tran Van Huong in a letter to Richard Critchfield of *The Washington Evening Star*, in which Huong estimated that as many as five million Vietnamese would be singled out for reprisals should the Communists gain control of the South. In his opinion, one million members of the South Vietnamese armed forces, 700,000 civil servants and their families, "and all those who have, one way or another, opposed Communist rule since 1945, will be subjected to reprisals, in spite of any guarantee that may be given them on paper." In commenting on the form that such reprisals might take, the former Prime Minister wrote: "Some may be eliminated physically, others may be jailed or sent to reeducation camps. At best, they will be treated as second-class citizens." In support of this view, he pointed to the experience of the Land Reform campaign in North Vietnam, where "hundreds of thousands of people were killed by the Communists."[17]

The existence of such perceptions may explain, in part, why the current GVN leaders are so adamantly opposed to any coalition government. Simply put, they are extremely reluctant to share power with those whom they believe to be their mortal enemies and who, they are convinced, only want to use a coalition as a stepping-stone to achieving complete control over the South, with all that this implies. Their attitude was perhaps most succinctly summed up by former President Ky, when he reportedly said about the prospects for reconciliation: "I regard the Communists as traitors and they regard me as a traitor. If I catch them I'll shoot them, and if they catch me they'll shoot me."[18]

These fears also suggest that, in any attempt at a negotiated settlement, GVN officials may manifest an overriding concern for ensuring their own physical security and that of their families. Thus, they would probably insist on retaining immediate and direct control over enough military and police forces to ensure such protection. Indeed, one could argue that, if these GVN leaders were forced to choose between accepting a coalition government which left considerable uncertainty as to who would control South Vietnam in the coming years and acceding to a territorial compromise that involved the neutralization or cession of part of their country to North Vietnam, they might well opt for the latter.

Finally, perceptions such as the above bear directly on the problem of maintaining the cohesion and morale of South Vietnam during the negotiations. For, as was mentioned earlier, the Viet Cong frequently offer their targets the explicit choice of either continuing their opposition to the Revolution and risking eventual repression, or joining the Revolution and earning clemency, and perhaps even reward, from the Communists. The proffer of clemency is the carrot that accompanies the stick of repression. But to merit it, GVN followers usually are required to atone for past "crimes" and demonstrate the sincerity of their new allegiance by performing some positive service for the Revolution; they may be asked to serve as fifth-columnists, or to provide intelligence to the Viet Cong, or even, in some cases, to assassinate their own colleagues.

Though we cannot assess the extent to which this carrot-and-stick approach has succeeded in subverting the present GVN structure, we must assume that it has not been without some effect. Indeed, it is entirely possible that there has already been considerable erosion at some levels of the civilian and military bureaucracy and that significant numbers of persons, particularly at lower echelons, are now acceding to Viet Cong demands. Still others may be attempting to "straddle"—i.e., to maintain secret contacts with Communists but at the same time to refrain from performing the kind of services that would irretrievably compromise them with the GVN.

But even with this uncertainty, it seems clear that enemy proselytizing efforts have not achieved the high levels of subversion for which they were aiming. Many captured documents contain statements to this effect and stress the need for greater efforts from civilian and military proselytizing cadres. One may speculate that a major reason why the carrot-and-stick approach has not had more success until now is that, in present circumstances, the alternatives posed by the Viet Cong simply do not have compelling credibility for most GVN officials. Many individuals either do not place much credence in Communist promises of clemency, or, perhaps more important, remain unpersuaded of the likelihood that the Viet Cong will be in a position to carry out their threats of repression. They see the over-all trend of the war as in the government's favor, and believe that U.S. and GVN forces will continue to provide adequate security for them and their families.

As the negotiations progress, however, the Viet Cong can be expected to intensify their campaign to secure defections from GVN ranks by predicting that the United States will in the end abandon South Vietnam and by warning individual targets that they *must act soon if they are to be of service to the Revolution and thus to merit clemency*. Many persons will continue to reject such an appeal because collaboration with the Communists is to them unthinkable. For others, a critical consideration will be their estimate of U.S. intentions. If this group came to believe that an abrupt American disengagement was imminent and that *the GVN's future capability to contain the enemy was in serious doubt*, their propensity to insure themselves with the Viet Cong would greatly increase. And should this occur on any significant scale, it would obviously have a most pernicious effect on the South Vietnamese government's capacity for continued resistance.

Cease-Fire

At some future point, the parties now contending in Vietnam may find it to their mutual interest to enter into some kind of cease-fire arrangement. While several different cease-fire configurations are possible, including *de facto* arrangements covering individual geographic areas, one possibility would be a formal, nationwide cessation of the fighting which would leave opposing forces *in situ* and would be regarded as a major step toward an eventual political settlement.

The Communists' behavior during any such cease-fire, including the decision whether or not to observe particular provisions of the agreement, would depend in large part on their assessment of the political-military situation obtaining at the time, and on their expectations as to the kind of settlement that might flow from the cease-fire and the penalties they might incur should they violate it. Thus, it is possible to imagine circumstances in which the Communists would place such a high value on the preservation of a cease-fire that they would refrain from any activities (including assassinations and abductions) which might cause the arrangement to break down. It is also possible, however, to postulate circumstances in which the Communists would choose to continue their campaign of repression in a cease-fire. In adopting such a course in spite of the risks involved, they would be motivated, above all, by the desire 1) to solidify control over areas under their domination at the time of the cease-fire, 2) to establish control in areas that were still disputed, 3) to prevent the GVN from increasing its presence in such contested areas, and 4) to promote their major objective, the capture of political power through the paralysis and disintegration of the government structure in Saigon and other urban centers.

Repression could become a particularly important factor in the contested areas, where the Viet Cong might believe themselves at a significant advantage over the government, as their covert and disciplined village organization could more easily circumvent the cease-fire than could the overt and cumbersome GVN institutions. The Communists, therefore, might be tempted to continue many of their repressive activities, including the assassination or abduction of local government officials and cadres, with the aim of demoralizing and paralyzing local government personnel. By forcing GVN officials to "keep their heads down" during the cease-fire period, the Viet Cong could hope to open the contested areas to intensive Communist organizational and political activities. They might look upon assassinations as particularly effective in countering any attempts by the government to push ahead with the nonmilitary (economic and social-welfare) aspects of its pacification program during the cease-fire. Another major aim of repression would be to persuade villagers of the government's impotence and inability to provide security even under conditions of a cease-fire, and at the same time to convince them that the Viet Cong's presence was permanent, and that there was no alternative to cooperating with the Revolution.

Similarly, the Viet Cong might continue repressive operations in urban and other GVN-controlled areas during a cease-fire as a way of maintaining pressure on the GVN structure, undermining morale, and facilitating Communist proselytizing efforts within the government's civilian and military bureaucracies. They might perceive improved opportunities for their assassination teams in these areas if a cease-fire were to mean greater ease of movement from rural to urban areas.

The Viet Cong might conclude that under a cease-fire repressive activities such as those outlined above would entail minimal risk. They might believe that they could take refuge behind their covert infrastructure, that their opponents would find it difficult to trace assassinations to their organization conclusively, and that villagers would be afraid to report incidents. More important, they might be convinced that the Allies, reluctant to terminate the cease-fire simply because of such incidents, would be constrained from taking retaliatory actions by the fear of being held responsible should the cease-fire break down.

While any discussion of possible Communist behavior during a cease-fire must of necessity be speculative, there is evidence in the captured documents to suggest that the Viet Cong may indeed be planning on a continuation of repressive activities under a cease-fire. The aforementioned Top Secret directive issued by the Security Section of Region II in 1967, for example, states that, "until the complete liberation" of the cities, the "struggle against spies and reactionaries" will continue and that, even when *the military warfare is provisionally over,* espionage should not decrease" but "will be intensified and will become more terrible and complicated." Here is the relevant portion of the directive in full:

To step up various activities in cities is the most important mission at present. From now until the complete liberation, the struggle between the enemy and ourselves in the cities will be more violent, protracted, and complicated. Although the revolution will pass into new phases, our struggle against spies and reactionaries and our protection of the movements are always very hard. *Cities are always important bases of the struggle against spies and reactionaries. As soon as the military warfare is provisionally over, espionage should not decrease. It will be intensified and will become more terrible and complicated.* [19]

The directive went on to urge that covert forces (including "security and secret agent networks") be developed in the cities to serve "immediate and long-range requirements" and prepare conditions for "the liberation of the cities."

A circular issued by Subregion 3 on November 26, 1968, which outlined the measures that local Viet Cong units should institute to counter the GVN's accelerated pacification program and Phuong Hoang (Phoenix) operations, contained explicit references to a possible cease-fire. The GVN's "new pacification plan" was said to be designed to gain "widespread control over the population in rural areas . . . particularly areas under mixed control prior to a cease-fire," and the GVN allegedly planned to utilize its Phuong Hoang organization to "find every way to annihilate all [Communist] underground cadres upon the declaration of the cease-fire." To counter these schemes, the circular directed that subordinate elements intensify the "security maintenance movement among the people" so as to discover GVN "intelligence and public security agents" and be prepared to "exterminate saboteurs when the cease-fire occurs." It went on to urge that local Viet Cong elements

Quickly consolidate forces of the security, armed reconnaissance, and espionage agencies and those reconnaissance agents in charge of protecting political activities and secret supporters in the villages, so that we can promptly detect and annihilate them [GVN agents and security personnel] presently and at the cease-fire. [20]

In light of the above, it would seem prudent, in the formulation of any cease-fire arrangements, to give consideration to the specific problem of repression. In the first place, a cease-fire agreement ought to contain explicit provisions proscribing all assassinations and abductions and to make it clear that such incidents would be construed as serious violations of the arrangement. It would also be desirable to develop contingency plans for the maintenance of security in GVN-controlled and contested areas (particularly with regard to the protection of government personnel in the conduct of their official duties) during a cease-fire and to consider possible countermeasures in the event of Communist violations. One response that might merit consideration would be the position that any significant incidence of assassinations or abductions in a contested area would *necessitate and justify* the introduction of additional GVN security forces. This might serve to nullify the psychological impact of such repressive activities and perhaps deter the Communists from attempting a quick takeover of contested areas.

Elections

Repression may also pose serious problems should any attempts be made in the next few years to conduct nationwide free elections (internationally supervised or not) to determine the future political complexion of South Vietnam. As in the case of a cease-fire, the behavior of the Communists during such elections cannot be predicted with any certainty, as it would again depend in large part on their analysis of the over-all political-military situation and on their expectations as to the outcome of the ballot. However, an examination of past Viet Cong policies and behavior may yield important indications of how the Communists might attempt to employ repressive instruments in a future election if they became convinced that repression was both necessary and polically advisable.

In the first place, it should be noted that "reactionary" political organizations have traditionally been prime targets for repression. A security directive issued in December 1965, for example, listed among the major targets to be repressed those "elements who actively counter the Revolution" and who are to be found "in different reactionary parties" such as the VNQDD, Dai Viet, and Can Lao. Particular attention was to be paid to the "core reactionary agents" who operated in the various political associations "formed by the puppet administration and the U.S." Also targeted for repression were the "reactionary elements" who "operated in various associations" and "exploited different religions such as Buddhism, Cao Daism, Protestantism, and Catholicism to counter the Revolution."[21] One Top Secret directive stated that security elements in the "large" provincial cities had to "struggle to exterminate the heads of political and reactionary organizations who are waiting for an opportunity to jump into the direct sabotage of our movement."[22] Another, concerning the "mission of eliminating traitors and tyrants" in the critical rural areas, stipulated that the major targets for repression were to include "reactionary factions and parties"; "key henchmen of the reactionary political organizations"; "the reactionaries working under the name of religion"; and former "party members who still oppose our actions and prevent the local movement."[23]

The captured documents also provide ample evidence that rank-and-file political party members as well as the leaders of political organizations are subject to assassination or abduction and that, when such persons fall into Viet Cong hands, they usually are either incarcerated in thought-reform camps or executed. A roster of persons arrested in various villages of Duc Pho District, Quang Ngai Province, from 1965 to early 1967, for example, contained the names of some forty-eight who were suspected of having "committed crimes" by being members of or closely associated with the VNQDD Party.[24] Other rosters, maintained by district thought-reform camps in Phu Yen Province, listed the names of numerous VNQDD, Dai Viet, and Can Lao members who had been executed or sentenced to from one to three years' imprisonment. Among those from the Dai Viet Party who were incarcerated or executed were a clerk from a district Party headquarters (24 months), a farmer who had "opposed the Revolution" (18 months), an individual who had "joined the reactionary" Party and had refused to stand trial (he was "killed on the spot"), and a provincial Party leader who had been "sentenced" on the spot [executed?] after an investigation." The rosters also included persons who were not formally members but were accused of having "constant relations with the Dai Viet gang."[25]

Party members also are subject to abduction. The notebook of a cadre from the Duy Xuyen District Security Section, Quang Da Province, with entries dated between June 1966 and April 1968, claimed that an average of ten persons were kidnapped by the Security Service in each village of the district every month, and that most of these were members of political organizations (such as the VNQDD, Dai Viet, and Can Lao), followers of various religions, or local GVN officials. According to the notebook, some of these victims had been secretly killed after capture while others had been publicly executed for their "antirevolutionary activities."[26]

The elimination of "reactionary" parties was also one of the objectives laid down for the General Offensive and General Uprising. According to a letter dated February 8, 1968, one of the explicit purposes of the mass uprising in the towns and cities was to bring about the destruction of pro-GVN political associations.[27] There is strong evidence that officials and members of political parties were major targets during the Tet attacks in and around the city of Hue; according to one Communist report, 145 leaders and rank-and-file members (113 of them VNQDD, 19 Dai Viet, and 13 Can Lao members) were killed or captured in the Hue area during the month of February. Of those reported killed, 50 belonged to the VNQDD, 7 were Dai Viet Party members, and 13 were associated with the Can Lao.[28] The high attrition of VNQDD personnel in the Hue area was confirmed on March 9, 1968, by a spokesman of that party who reported that "dozens" of VNQDD members "had been executed by the Communists during their occupation of Hue, including four members of the Party's central committee, one of whom, Professor Pham Dinh Bach, was Secretary General of the Party." According to the same source, "hundreds of the Party's members and local leaders in the suburbs of Hue and in Thua Thien Province" were missing and "feared to have been killed, abducted or forced to flee their villages during the Communist offensive."[29] It also should be noted that the Communists executed "one of the five elected National Assembly Senators from Hue" during their occupation of that city.[30]

Some idea of the intensity with which VNQDD officials and members are pursued by the Communists can be garnered from a directive entitled "On the Strong Repression of Nationalist Party [VNQDD] Members," issued by a Viet Cong agency in Quang Ngai Province on March 29, 1968. This directive, which was classified Secret, claimed that during "the recent General Offensive and General Uprising . . . we killed 96 wicked tyrants, captured 148 others" and compelled 90 Nationalist Party members "to resign from their party and flee to various provinces." The directive nevertheless urged local agencies to place even "more emphasis on the liquidation of Nationalist [Party] ringleaders and the disintegration, from top to bottom, of their various organizations." It ordered local units to

Carefully investigate the offices of the Nationalist Party at district, province, town, and village levels.

Get an accurate estimate of its [Nationalist Party] strength.

Make appropriate plans so that "suicide units" are able to suppress the Nationalist ringleaders who are considered "wicked tyrants."

Strive to liquidate, as soon as possible, Nationalist Party followers who are living in various cities and towns and who have incurred a blood debt. [31]

The aim was to force the Nationalist Party's organization within the province into complete stagnation by July 1968:

We must try to carry out this plan so that in June 1968, all district and village Nationalist Party Committees will be frightened and will shirk their duties and in July 1968, the province Nationalist Party Committees will be unable to motivate the Party members and the Party will become stagnant. [32]

Another pattern of Viet Cong activity which may have relevance for any future elections in the South are the attempts of the Communists to disrupt GVN elections in the past and to repress persons who are brought into office by ballot. Mainly, they have tried to dissuade local populations from voting and to intimidate potential candidates. Prior to the 1966 Constituent Assembly elections, for example, the Communists mounted an "anti-election movement" aimed specifically at holding down the vote. According to a Top Secret report issued by the Saigon-Gia Dinh Region Party Committee after the elections, the movement in Saigon had succeeded beyond "expectations," as large numbers of voters had been persuaded to boycott the elections. But the report noted that "many deficiencies still existed" in the anti-election movement:

... we did not succeed in countering spies, killing members of the tyrant circle. ... In particular, our armed activities were decreased a day before the election. On election day, basically no subversive activities were carried out. While the enemy forces were concentrated at polling stations, we did not take advantage of this to conduct meetings with the people, to break the enemy grip, and to counter the enemy spies in labor hamlets which were completely abandoned. [33]

The report urged that the "political struggle" against the Constituent Assembly be intensified and that, among other things, local units strive to "continuously punish ringleader Vietnamese traitors in the Assembly as a threat to all its members." [34]

The Viet Cong also mounted a concerted campaign to disrupt the village and hamlet elections in the spring of 1967. In some areas, they explicitly threatened repression to deter persons from seeking candidacy and from participating in the organization of the ballot. On March 18, for example, the People's Liberation Front Committee for Quang Nam Province issued an "Order" which "absolutely" forbade anyone to offer himself as a candidate in hamlet and village elections, and directed those already on candidate rolls to withdraw. Two of the articles of the Order read:

Article III. The people are forbidden to participate in hamlet and village elections being organized by the puppet government. No one is allowed to come close to the polls.

Article IV. Those who organize the elections and those who do not obey the Front's order and present themselves as candidates will be indicted on a charge of being accomplices of the tyrannical, reactionary henchmen and will be punished.

The Front is not liable for the loss of life of those who come near the polls.[35]

Viet Cong "armed forces, paramilitary forces for liberation, security agencies and popular organizations of the Front" were to see the execution of the various proscriptions laid down in the Order.[36]

Repression was particularly widespread during the campaign and poll that preceded the presidential and senatorial elections of September 3, 1967. Viet Cong units attempted to assassinate or kidnap GVN employees who were helping to organize the electoral campaign; they tried to seize voter registration and identification cards, and to intimidate local populations into boycotting the elections by warning them in propaganda sessions "that those who participated in the elections would be sent to a thought-reform camp for six months to one year.[37] One Communist document, captured in Nhon Trach District, Bien Hoa Province, stated:

We must continuously attack the enemy in all fields so as to crush [his] plot of launching a two-pronged attack and defeat the so-called "Presidential election. ..." The September struggle phase is aimed at demolishing the deceitful "Presidential" election comedy. ... From now to the enemy "Presidential election day," guerrilla forces are to search out and destroy early any group that propagandizes and advertises the enemy's tricky so-called election comedy.

On election day, guerrilla forces are to stick to and attack at any price all enemy groups that force people to go to the polls and disperse people that are gathered by the enemy; the secret self-defense members are to be ready to attack right at the polling stations or operate in coordination with the guerrillas to destroy ballot boxes and punish the tyrants. ...[38]

None of these attempts to disrupt GVN elections succeeded to any significant degree—indeed, during the presidential elections a high percentage of the registered voters went to the polls—largely because of the tight security measures instituted by the GVN and other Allied forces. Yet the use of repression in this context has not been without effect, particularly on village and hamlet elections, where the Viet Cong's ability to assassinate or abduct candidates is most credible. During the 1969 village and hamlet elections, for example, there were reports that the government had been unable to find enough candidates for the available positions "in many communities." This was directly attributed to the fact that the Viet Cong "have made politics—at least government-affiliated politics—a dangerous business in the countryside."[39] According to one press report, a hamlet chief who was running for reelection in the mountain resort town of Dalat was assassinated two days before the election and no other candidate would come forward to fill his place. Commenting on this incident, a senior U.S. adviser in the area said: "The people are afraid. There have been too many assassinations, no one wants the job."[40]

In view of these examples of Communist activity, the security requirements for a properly supervised and truly free ballot to determine the future political destiny of the South would have to be very stringent indeed. This applies not only to the electoral campaign and the ballot itself *but also to the preelection organizational phase and the postelection period.*

It has been suggested, for example, that, in looking toward the possibility of such elections, the government, with the aid of various political parties and religious sects, may attempt to establish some kind of grass-roots political organization in the South. If previous behavior is any guide, there is a strong probability that the Communists would adamantly contest such a move and would immediately target their repressive instruments on the officials and workers associated with the new organization, much as they did with members of the Dai Viet and VNQDD parties. A similar response might await any other nongovernmental but anti-Communist political party that attempted to mount a major organizational drive in the countryside. It should be noted that the Security Service maintains a careful watch over all new "reactionary" parties or political groupings in the South and gives high priority to the collection of intelligence on the operations, policies, and personnel of such organizations.[41]

The problem of security is directly relevant to the postelectoral period as well. Over the years, the Viet Cong have established a high credibility, both in "liberated" and in many contested areas, for their capacity to *identify and repress* villagers who act against the wishes of the Revolution. This factor could decisively influence the vote of many thousands of Vietnamese, should they come to believe that after elections they would be left vulnerable to Viet Cong retribution.

Finally, there remain the many problems of ensuring an open campaign and free ballot: the protection of candidates, an adequate flow of election information to the hamlets, and the unimpeded movement of voters to the polls. In short, truly free and open elections in the South will require security measures and forces far in excess of the few thousand international poll-watchers that some observers have suggested.

The Prospects for Local Accommodation

It has been argued that one way in which peace might come to Vietnam would be through a growing accommodation between GVN and Viet Cong leaders at the local level. Some observers believe that significant instances of such accommodation already exist in the South, and that, with the proper encouragement, this could become the pattern for the country as a whole. Robert Shaplen, for example, suggests that important segments from the lower levels of the Viet Cong structure might be induced to break with their parent organization and desist from further armed struggle in return for guarantees of local autonomy and an opportunity to "maintain a voice for themselves in the countryside" through a process of hamlet and village self-rule. He further points out that a framework for accommodation has been established in a number of areas in Vietnam "where tacit cease-fires already exist between Communist and government forces, each agreeing to leave the other alone."[42]

Granted that the proponents of this view are by no means insensitive to the many difficulties entailed in nurturing widespread accommodation in the South, it may be useful to emphasize some of the larger obstacles to such a development. An analysis of captured documents and the Viet Cong campaign of repression raises some serious doubts about it on several counts.

In the first place, one must be cautious in extrapolating from what appear to be existing patterns of accommodation. In many instances, they simply reflect a condition of mutual weakness, where neither side possesses the organization, resources, or motivation to contest the presence of the other. General Westmoreland, for example, has suggested that it was the political instability in Saigon which in 1964 led local government officials in many outlying areas—especially in the Delta—to reach "tacit agreements with the Viet Cong and Communist infrastructure to 'live and let live'," and that "the same was true of many Regional and Popular Force commanders in remote outposts."[43]

There is also reason to believe, however, that much of the accommodation which exists at these levels is asymmetrical, in that it benefits the local units or organization of the Viet Cong more than it does the GVN's. Thus, in those contested villages where the GVN still maintains outposts but where the forces garrisoning these posts are relatively passive ("motionless," to use the Viet Cong's own word), with little attempt to harass their Communist counterparts, the Viet Cong generally are free to exact what they want from the villagers: to collect taxes, recruit manpower and laborers, and carry out needed organizational activities. In 1968, for example, during their drive to establish "People's Administrative Councils" in the hamlets and villages, Viet Cong authorities directed that "Village Liberation People's Councils" be elected even in "villages where there are enemy posts, but which are tightly surrounded by our forces, and where our Party Chapters, organizations and guerrillas are still strong."[44] In many such contested villages, the Viet Cong consider the GVN's presence to be effectively neutralized and are reluctant to upset the existing situation, lest, in trying to overrun the GVN outposts, they draw unwanted attention to the area or cause the villages to be garrisoned by stronger and much more aggressive government forces.

Many instances of accommodation in the countryside apparently are asymmetrical also in the sense that, while they have resulted from a conscious policy decision on the part of higher Viet Cong authorities, this probably has not been the case with the local GVN units or officials involved. The captured documents contain explicit orders to Viet Cong commanders not to take military initiatives against GVN units that prove "passive" or appear "to some extent divided from Saigon," but instead to attempt to proselytize the personnel serving in such units. A "Guideline for the 1966-67 Troop Proselytizing Task" issued by COSVN on October 30, 1966, for example, includes this passage:

With those enemy units which proved passive in sweep operations, non-coopera-tive to the Americans, discontent with both the U.S. and puppets, or to some extent divided from Saigon, we should attempt to establish contact. If they

*really want peace, [and] do not seek to terrorize the people or destroy our
movement. . . we will not take the initiative against them but will use political
propaganda and motivation instead.* Our task will vary according to time and
place, so that we can work for the benefit of the people and the Revolution and
can consolidate our weak areas.

This policy should be realized at any price, and we should meet the basic
requirements of troop proselytizing. An indistinct conception of the task will
lead us toward rightism and loss of [a correct] standpoint. The utmost
flexibility is also necessary. This policy is aimed at isolating the U.S. to the
greatest extent possible and depriving them of any military support. *Our
propaganda and motivation will create an atmosphere of passiveness, some
degree of neutrality, or possibly even cooperation from the enemy posts,* and we
should take advantage of any opportunities to rush the enemy soldiers and
officers to the revolutionary side. In the course of events, we should try to
infiltrate some of our men who can win over the people and soldiers and work
for the disintegration of [puppet] units.[45]

Other captured directives also suggest that the Communists often
pursue a policy of simply encouraging local GVN units or posts to
remain "stationary and neutral" and thereby abstain from sweep
operations.[46] Many cases of supposed local accommodation, then,
appear to be but temporary and fragile arrangements which the Viet
Cong consider to be of benefit to their side, and which they are
prepared to break whenever it is in their interest to do so.

A second reason for doubting the likelihood of widespread mutual
accommodation is that a major thrust of Viet Cong policy in the
rural areas has been to prevent any real accommodation from
developing between government and Communist forces. As has been
shown, once the Communists establish a strong presence in an area,
they try to seal off the local population from any further contact
with the government side. Indeed, their policy is to polarize the
population, to induce it to "accept no coexistence" with the GVN,
and to maintain the sharpest possible line between those who
support the Revolution and those who oppose it. This policy is
manifest in the numerous indoctrination sessions devoted to "deep-
ening the people's hatred" of the GVN and to inciting them to
vindictive action against government persons by detailing the many
"blood debts" that GVN officials and other "tyrants" allegedly owe
them. It is also apparent in the Viet Cong's use of "People's Courts"
for the public trial of "spies" and "counterrevolutionaries" as a way
of impressing local populations with the Revolution's firm attitude
toward those who cooperate with the GVN. The same policy
accounts for the practice of keeping under surveillance, and if need

be repressing, any villagers who manifest a lack of sympathy for the Revolution or who are suspected of maintaining contact with persons associated with the GVN, even if they are close relatives. The harsh treatment of suspected GVN spies and agents in rural areas is at least partly designed to dissuade villagers from treating with the government in any way.

This "absolutist" policy toward nonrevolutionary elements at the local levels also showed itself in the way in which the Viet Cong went about establishing their "People's Administrative Councils" in "liberated" and contested areas during 1968. In ordering the formation of these local administrations, the Communists took pains to emphasize the critical difference between the tactical expedience of their advocacy of relatively broad-based coalitions at the central government level and in the large cities, and the kind of absolutist revolutionary administrations they sought at the provincial, district, and village levels. A directive attributed to the Current Affairs Committee of Subregion 3 said about this difference:

The revolutionary administration is a legal and "absolutist" tool for the implementation of the national and democratic revolution, the immediate objective of which [is] to defeat the lackey administration and the U.S. will of aggression, and firmly punish the antirevolutionaries. Therefore, one should not be misled by the broad-based coalition at the upper level into entertaining vague notions about the "class absolutism" nature of the revolutionary administration, and committing rightist errors. [47]

Another directive, also emanating from Subregion 3, described the mission of the revolutionary administration as follows:

Being a Legal Dictatorial Instrument, it must help complete the present democratic national revolutionary phase. At first we should smash the aggressive will of the U.S. imperialists and their lackeys, and *resolutely punish the antirevolutionary individuals*. For this reason, when seeing the broad coalition of the government at high level, we should not forget the (proletarian) class dictatorship nature of the revolutionary administration and commit the mistake of bending ourselves towards rightism.

The revolutionary administration must fully display its revolutionary characteristics because it has been established on the foundation of the Vietnamese people's sacrifices, hardships, and gallantry. It should resolutely defeat all enemy counteroffensive plans, *oppress all antirevolutionary remnant elements*, maintain the achievements of the Revolution, develop and strengthen the people's [supremacy]. [48]

The directive went on to say that "the Party should perform its absolute role in the leadership of the revolutionary administrative organizations." In villages where Party members were numerous, "Party members must occupy two-thirds of the total number of [Village] Council seats." Even in newly-liberated areas, where Party members were few, a number sufficient "to insure good leadership of the Party" were to be appointed.[49] The directive, like the one cited just before, emphasized that one of the primary missions of the new revolutionary administrations was to overthrow the "lackey's clique" and "to repress and punish the reactionaries."

A third major impediment to the development of local accommodation on any significant scale is the ubiquitous Viet Cong Security Service, which is organized down to the village level and possesses a vast network of secret agents and informants in both rural and urban areas. One of the primary functions of this security apparatus is to keep watch over and ensure the political reliability of all cadres and personnel in the Viet Cong infrastructure. To this end, security cadres maintain files on persons in local Viet Cong organizations whom they consider potentially unreliable or subject to ideological deviations, and they are prepared to move swiftly and firmly against those who step out of line.

The need for close surveillance over all personnel, including Party members, is constantly emphasized, as in the instructions to subordinate echelons in a Top Secret COSVN security directive of November 1966:

Conduct searching investigations within our own ranks. Attention is to be focused first on individuals with poor records. The investigation of such individuals must be carefully conducted. Unit commanders must know each and every cadre and man under their command.[50]

A January 1967 directive from Quang Nam Province echoed the same theme, as it urged various Party and Group chapters within the province to investigate the political viewpoints of every member, and request all military units to do the same, as a way of discovering the poorly motivated.[51]

It is important to note that all echelons of the Viet Cong bureaucracy are subject to such surveillance—including the most senior officials—and that Security Section chiefs at every level enjoy the unique prerogative of bypassing regular Party channels and reporting directly to higher echelons any questionable behavior or attitudes on the part of their immediate colleagues. It should also be remembered that the Security Service maintains strong and unique ties to the Ministry of Public Security (MPS) in North Vietnam, both because many of its key posts are held by MPS officials who have been infiltrated from the North and because each echelon above district level is at times subject to direct orders from the Ministry.

The very existence of this security apparatus would therefore appear to constitute a major barrier to any widespread unauthorized contact or cooperation between Viet Cong cadres and local GVN officials.[52] One would assume, for example, that the Security Service would not tolerate for long a Viet Cong village organization which attempted to enter into an *independent* arrangement with the local GVN structure. Indeed, it is highly probable that the Security Service, upon discovering such a development, would immediately dispatch an Armed Reconnaissance Unit to the village concerned and would attempt to punish every one of the local cadres who had promoted the arrangement. In short, as long as this efficient security apparatus remains intact, accommodation of this sort in the South will be very difficult, always assuming, of course, that Communist policy continues to oppose it.

Furthermore, one has to reckon with existing perceptions on both sides that stem from the length and the ferocity of the war. Not only do the South Vietnamese fear the retribution awaiting them in case of a Communist take-over, but many Viet Cong cadres probably have similarly pessimistic expectations as to what might happen to them should they fall into the hands of the GVN. For, just as the GVN official can point to years of sustained Communist repression in the South, so the Viet Cong cadre can point to the Allies' current Phuong Hoang (Phoenix) operations. Aimed at the elimination (by capture, defection, or death) of the Viet Cong infrastructure from its center down to village and hamlet level, the Phuong Hoang system seeks to collate all available intelligence on local Viet Cong organizations, so that Allied military forces and such paramilitary ones as the National Police Field Forces, the National Police Special Branch, and the Provincial Reconnaissance Units may systematically track down individual cadres within that infrastructure.

Similarly, just as GVN persons may fear a repetition of the Land Reform campaign in the North, many Viet Cong cadres no doubt recall the repression of former Viet Minh in much of the countryside during the early years of the Diem regime. Even though this was on a much smaller and far less bloody scale than the Land Reform in the North, it appears to have been sufficiently widespread and intense to lead many Southern cadres to regard any future "promises of amnesty with cynicism, and to fear for their lives if their side is not victorious."[53] Indeed, in the words of one analyst, "the argument that the leadership in Communist North Vietnam treated its opponents with even greater brutality than did the government in the South is likely, if anything, to reinforce the [Viet Cong's] fears about their fate in a future settlement."[54] Evidence of this distrust is to be found in the Communists' own testimony, which shows that, particularly for the hard-core Viet Cong, one of the major deterrents to defection or surrender continues to be the fear of mistreatment or execution by the GVN. Mutual perceptions such as these would in themselves block the way to local accommodation on a large scale.

Some Thoughts on the Likelihood of Repression Under a Communist Regime

Finally, it remains for us to examine the possible pattern of repression in the melancholy contingency that a Communist regime were to assume power in South Vietnam—that is to say, were to secure control over the central government as well as over the security forces (military and police) throughout the countryside. Would the bloody reprisals feared by so many GVN persons actually occur in such circumstances, or would the Communists, for reasons of political self-interest, adopt a policy of leniency toward their former adversaries and attempt to use a modicum of violence? Although any discussion of possible Communist behavior under such circumstances *must obviously be considered highly speculative*, it may be useful to examine some of the considerations that might influence the course of a Communist regime in this respect.

First of all, future policies toward the former enemies of the Revolution could in part be influenced by the manner in which the Communist regime gained power in the South. It should be remembered in this context that the Viet Cong leadership envisages as one of the most likely paths to final victory a series of General Offensives and General Uprisings of the kind attempted in 1968, wherein, through a sustained and intensive application of violence, they expect to break GVN control in both the urban and rural areas irrevocably. According to present doctrine, this would necessitate the systematic hunting down and annihilation of many thousands of government officials, civil servants, military leaders, "spies," and "reactionaries." Also, there probably would be a concerted effort to motivate the masses to "seethingly arise" and participate in the tracking down and extermination of these target groups. If the Communists were to gain control by this path—say, following a withdrawal of all U.S. military forces—one could expect a *"blood-bath" of very large proportions* simply in the process of their assuming power. The pattern of executions exhibited in the Hue area in February 1968 could be replicated throughout the country, and the momentum of such violence might well extend into the time when the new regime was attempting to consolidate its power.

If, on the other hand, the Communists were to win control by a different road—say, through the gradual subversion and eventual capture of a coalition government established under an international arrangement—then the likelihood of widespread violence at least *during the take-over period* might be significantly smaller. In the initial stages of such a coalition, political considerations might dicatate a conciliatory posture, causing the Communists to treat many of their former GVN targets cautiously lest the coalition break down and open warfare be resumed. According to this scenario, the Communists might choose to emphasize their civilian and military proselytizing activities; to rely on persuasion and inducements to win the support and allay the fears of the opposition; and to use violence only to the extent necessary to ensure their eventual control over the new government's non-Communist military and police forces. Exactly what the "extent necessary" would be is uncertain; much would depend on the degree to which today's civilian and military GVN officials would at that point attempt to oppose the Communists' gradual assumption of total power. If such opposition proved widespread or deep-seated (which is very possible), the Communists could be expected to come down hard on their adversaries, and there probably would be considerable bloodshed. If, on the other hand, they managed to achieve control without much violence, this experience in itself could temper their future behavior toward persons now associated with the GVN.

Still other considerations might mitigate the conduct of a Communist regime once it had assumed dominant control in the South. In the first place, a major argument for the repression of many groups who now constitute priority targets would no longer obtain; the disintegration of the GVN would be an accomplished fact, and the civilian and military officials who had formerly obstructed the Revolution would have been stripped of office and presumably neutralized. Similarly, that portion of the GVN structure which under conditions of warfare endangers the cohesion and security of the Communist movement (such as the cadres associated with the GVN's Chieu Hoi and psychological warfare programs), or which now challenges Viet Cong control in the contested areas (the Rural Development cadres, among others), would no longer pose an organized threat. In short, an important change of context would have occurred, and many of the persons who are targets for liquidation or imprisonment to a Communist movement struggling to gain power might be viewed in a somewhat different light by a regime that was in control. This would be particularly true of the Communists' attitude toward those former GVN officials and supporters who proved readily acquiescent and actively cooperative.

Once in power, a Communist regime would have to confront major new problems, including those of establishing an orderly administration throughout the country and rehabilitating a war-torn economy. Not the least of its problems would be how to forge a degree of unity and mobilize support in a society deeply fractured by prolonged warfare and embracing a number of diverse ethnic minorities and religious groups that are likely to be very apprehensive about their fate under the new regime. Any Communist government presumably would want to avoid actions that might hamper its major task of political consolidation and mobilization. It would want, in particular, to eschew the kind of indiscriminate mass reprisals that might permanently alienate much of the population (promote "deep dissension between the people and the Revolution"), or encourage widespread passive resistance, or even drive segments of religious and ethnic groups into open insurgency. To avoid such developments and to gain the initial goodwill of the population, the Communists might see merit in a policy of tolerance and leniency toward the large majority of those previously associated with the GVN, particularly the rank and file of the GVN's military and paramilitary force structure and persons who had served in nonsensitive echelons of the civilian bureaucracy. They would constitute an important source of manpower for the new regime, and many would possess needed technical skills. Similar considerations could lead the Communists to refrain from any broadside punitive actions against religious sects and ethnic minorities that have tended to side with the GVN or to oppose the Viet Cong in the course of the war. Indeed, they might even choose to keep in force, at least for a time, their present circumspect policy with regard to the repression of "hostile" religious and ethnic minority leaders.

A final consideration which might have a mitigating influence on the behavior of a future Communist regime would be the international response to a major bloodbath, particularly the possibility of adverse reactions in other Communist states or parties and among the uncommitted nations. It is even conceivable that the leaders of such a regime might fear some form of international sanctions, such as trade restrictions, should they go too far. Their concerns about foreign reactions would probably depend in part on the extent to which they thought they could conceal internal developments in the South from the outside. Therefore, the presence of a large and adequately chartered international supervisory body in the country might serve to inhibit mass reprisals, though one must keep in mind that the presence of the International Control Commission teams in North Vietnam after the 1954 Geneva settlement did little to prevent the widespread violence and terror of the Land Reform campaign.

While considerations such as those sketched above might serve to hold down the scale and intensity of postwar violence in the South, other interests and factors could lead a Communist regime in quite a different direction, persuading it to encourage, or at least permit, the widespread and violent repression of GVN persons and supporters who are now marked down as "enemies of the Revolution."

To begin with, a new regime might see such violence as essential to the consolidation of its control in the South. Any Communist government, having gathered the formal reins of power, would want to move swiftly to amplify and secure its control, particularly in those urban and rural areas which previously had been dominated by the GVN.[55] It would seek to establish forthwith the supremacy of the Party at all echelons of the country's administrative hierarchy, and probably would embark immediately upon the twofold task of conditioning the entire population to accept both the authority and the discipline of the Party and of preparing the "masses" for the economic and political policies that the Communists would deem essential to South Vietnam's movement toward "socialism" and the consummation of their Revolution.

In confronting this problem of consolidation, a new Communist regime might be sorely tempted to purge the population at the outset of those *hard-core* supporters of the government who by past behavior and outlook had shown themselves to be implacable enemies of the Revolution. Not only would such persons be considered of little value in a Communist society, but, more important, they would probably be viewed as a dangerous source of potential opposition—the "stubborn elements" who would "lie in wait to sabotage" the regime and its programs.

To judge by the testimony of the Viet Cong's own documents, substantial numbers of persons (already classified as "traitors," "tyrants," "reactionaries," "counterrevolutionaries," etc.) could fall into that category of hard-core resisters too dangerous to leave unattended. The Viet Cong see "stubborn elements" at all echelons of the present GVN civilian and military hierarchy—from the "cruel" hamlet and interfamily chiefs, village policemen, security agents, etc. who now operate at the local level, to the numerous "wicked" civilian officials and military commanders who occupy positions at district, province, and higher echelons of the GVN structure. A future, Communist government might well conclude that these remnants of the old regime could only be absorbed into a "socialist" state at an unacceptable risk, and that it would be advisable to remove them systematically from the new society, be it by physical elimination or through long-term incarceration in thought-reform camps. Such a Communist regime, therefore, might seek to "purify" the villages, towns, and cities of the South as a whole in much the same way as the Viet Cong now attempt to "cleanse" their liberated areas of persons they deem undesirable.

The Communists might see further advantages in such a purge. They could look on it as an effective warning to anyone who might be inclined to harbor "reactionary thoughts" and as a vehicle for impressing upon the population the "absolutist viewpoint" of the new regime toward all opposition. They might well believe that, if they adopted a lenient posture toward major former adversaries (having, after all, consistently labeled them "cruel" "wicked," or "tyrannical" during the struggle for power), the population might then question both the avowed aims of the Revolution and the kind of discipline to be expected from the new order. Such doubts, in turn, might embolden some potentially acquiescent people to withhold their cooperation or even actively to resist the new government.

To forestall such a development, the Communist leadership might choose to make examples of its most stubborn adversaries by bringing them before public denunciation sessions in the villages and city wards, where the ritual of condemnation, confession, and trial by a People's Court could be played out in front of large numbers of spectators. This would be quite consistent with the current Communist practice of establishing "People's Courts" in order to "eliminate reactionaries" in newly-liberated villages.[56] The regime might take a page from the Land Reform in the North and establish quotas for the minimum number of "tyrants" and "reactionaries" to be tried and liquidated in a given hamlet or urban area. (Again it should be remembered that the Viet Cong frequently set quotas for liquidations in the South today.)

But beyond these more pracitical considerations of control lies the important concept of crime and punishment, an intrinsic part of Vietnamese Communist doctrine, according to which whoever commits a serious crime against the Revolution or the "people" must either submit to the punishment of the Viet Cong or atone for his past actions by performing a concrete service for the Revolution. It will be remembered that all blacklists are supposed to specify the crimes of each target so that appropriate punishment can be levied once the person falls into Communist hands. Local Viet Cong security cadres, as we have seen, are constantly urged by higher authorities to "keep records of the wicked individuals and those who owe a blood debt to us" so that "we may properly convict them when we have liberated" the area. Evidence from captured security directives and blacklists strongly suggests that the Communists have every intention of holding those now labeled "criminals" accountable, once they have control of the South.

If this were to happen, many thousands of South Vietnamese, because of their past positions or their alleged crimes, could expect death or at least long prison terms. Among the categories of persons most in danger of such severe punishment would be the following:

Viet Cong defectors — particularly those who have provided useful intelligence to the GVN, have allowed themselves to be exploited for psychological warfare purposes, or have taken up arms against their former comrades. Among this group would be former Viet Cong who now man the GVN's Armed Propaganda Teams and those who serve Allied forces as Kit Carson Scouts.

Intelligence and counterintelligence personnel — including members of the Central Intelligence Organization, the Military Security Service, Census Grievance Teams, and the Hamlet Informant Program, plus the large numbers of other local agents and paid informants now in the active service of the GVN.

National Police and other security personnel — in particular those closely associated with the Phuong Hoang operations, aimed at eliminating the Viet Cong infrastructure: the National Police Field

Forces, the National Police Special Branch, and the Provincial Reconnaissance Units. Other members of the National Police, such as those serving in the Uniform and Patrol Branch, would also be vulnerable, as would the officials and cadres serving in the GVN Ministry of Interior, which has responsibility for administering the police and the country's judicial and penal systems.

Government officials — including senior officials of the central government as well as middle-ranking officials serving in the provinces and districts. There are also a great many local officials (such as hamlet and village administrative personnel) who have incurred "blood debts" in the eyes of the Viet Cong by allegedly extracting bribes or "ruthless taxes" from the people, "herding" civilians into strategic hamlets, or harassing and intimidating persons sympathetic to the Revolution.

Officers and noncommissioned officers — most vulnerable among them officers of field-grade rank and higher in the GVN's Regular and Regional Forces. But, as in the case of GVN officials, a large number of junior commissioned and senior noncommissioned officers from these forces would also be classified as "tyrants." The same would apply to many persons serving at the platoon- and squad-leader level in the CIDG, Popular Forces, and People's Self-Defense Forces.

Officials and members of "reactionary" political organizations — including, of course, Dai Viet and VNQDD Party members as well as persons who have been associated with the Can Lao.

Should a Communist regime in South Vietnam in fact decide to deal severely with persons from groups such as those listed above, as this author believes it would, the number of *executions alone* could well total many tens of thousands. One can only guess at what the *minimum* would be, but, given the size of the target categories involved, this author finds it difficult to believe that the number would be much less than 100,000. Indeed, it might well be considerably higher.

The chances that this could happen would seem to be strengthened by the highly emotional "hate campaigns" which the Viet Cong have waged against their adversaries throughout the war, in a concerted effort to "incite" the people's "wrath," to "arouse" their "hate," and to "heighten their concept of revenge" toward the enemies of the Revolution. Their policy has been, to quote the words of but one directive, to "make the people feel a profound hatred of [the] enemy's savage crimes and to incite them to avenge their compatriots and kinfolk." [57]

Thus, it is entirely possible that a desire for revenge could of itself foment widespread violence against former GVN persons in a Communist South Vietnam. This would be particularly true if a Communist regime were to allow its local cadres and supporters a "free hand" in punishing their former adversaries and thus settle scores accumulated over many years of ferocious warfare.[58] (It must be remembered in this context that the present conflict in the South has engendered far more violent antagonisms than did the Viet Minh's struggle against the French.) The concept of revenge is by no means alien to Vietnamese culture, where the actions of an individual that affect another person negatively often prompt sharp retaliation, ranging from the common practice of poison-pen letters to vendetta-style murders in the most serious cases. Even in the relatively close-knit society of the village, revenge is often sought for damage to one's property or person. The Vietnamese press is full of accounts of incidents involving revenge, including many love triangles in which the husband has killed a cheating wife and her lover, or where the wife has castrated her husband and disfigured his mistress with acid.[59]

In conclusion, it should be noted that the above discussion does not address itself to one other possibility—namely, that a Communist regime might, at some time, attempt a radical and rapid transformation of society (including collectivization) by fostering in the South the kind of grass-roots violence that was employed in the North during the Land Reform campaign of the 1950s. If this were to happen, the addition of the "landlords" (including numerous small landowners, if the pattern of the North were followed) and of the mercantile ("comprador") class would swell the number of potential victims, and the likelihood of an extensive bloodbath would be very great indeed.

Notes

Chapter 1
Introduction

1. Each captured document used in this study will be cited by the identifying "Document Log" (Doc. Log) number officially assigned to it by the CDEC.

2. *The Washington Post*, August 28, 1969, p. A-23.

3. The captured documents cited in this study came from Communist agencies in 7 of the 8 Military Regions and in 26 of the 37 Communist Provinces and Subregions. The originating echelons include Communist political and military organizations at the COSVN, Region, Province, District, and Village level.

Chapter 2
The Targets and Purposes of Repression

1. From the newspaper *Thoi-Luan*, December 15, 1957, as quoted in Bernard B. Fall, "South Viet-Nam's Internal Problems," *Pacific Affairs*, September 1958, p. 257.

2. Fall, *ibid*.

3. Among the most authoritative and comprehensive of these is Doc. Log No. 07-1770-67 (Confidential), dated November 8, 1967, which provides translations of three lengthy security directives (in draft form) produced by the Security Section of Region II in the spring of 1967. The first directive, dated April 25, 1967, concerns "the intensification of the struggle against spies and reactionaries in various cities"; the second, the problem of "mastering the counter-espionage activities of the Party in critical rural areas"; and the third focuses on "the strengthening of the leadership of Party Committee levels and Village Party Chapters and on stepping up the struggle against spies and reactionaries in liberated and disputed areas." All three directives are classified Top Secret; they were circulated by Region II to subordinate echelons on May 18, 1967, and captured by elements of the RVNAF IV CTZ on June 20, 1967. Another important source is Doc. Log No. 10-1679-66 (Confidential), dated March 13, 1967, which contains a translation of a directive (on "measures" to be taken "to deal with reactionary elements") apparently issued by a high-level Viet Cong security agency on December 24, 1965. Attached to this directive was a second security document, relating to "Reform Indoctrination." Both documents were captured by the 1st U.S. Air Cavalry Division on October 3, 1966.

4. Doc. Log No. 10-1679-66 (see n. 3).

5. For example, Doc. Log No. 03-2556-68 (Confidential), dated May 21, 1968. Translation of an after-action report which assesses various Communist operations during the 1968 General Offensive in Saigon. Captured by the 199th U.S. Light Infantry Brigade on March 21, 1968.

6. Doc. Log No. 01-2289-69 (Confidential), dated January 30, 1969 (emphasis added). Translation of "Directive No. 169.AN" on the "nature, functions, missions, development, organization, training, daily activity and combat activity of armed reconnaissance units in the areas which border cities." The directive was prepared by the Security Section of COSVN and was addressed to the Security Sections of Subregions 1 and 4. Captured by the C/1/RAR, 1st ATF, on January 19, 1969.

7. Doc. Log No. 06-1939-69 (Confidential), dated August 11, 1969. Translation of a Secret directive dated May 18, 1969 (concerning the "pressing and specific requirements of missions to be accomplished by various security branches") believed to have been issued by an agency of the Can Duoc District Unit, Subregion 3. Captured by the 9th U.S. Infantry Division on June 17, 1969.

8. *Ibid.*

9. Doc. Log No. 07-1770-67 (see n. 3).

10. *Ibid.*

11. *Ibid.*, emphasis added.

12. Doc. Log No. 04-1687-68 (Confidential), summarized in MACJ2 Bulletin No. 11,182, April 9, 1968. Summary of a plan, dated November 25, 1967, and attributed to a commander in Rung Sat Special Zone, Subregion 4, providing guidance for village-level activities. Captured by RTAVR on March 20, 1968.

13. Doc. Log No. 10-2187-68 (Confidential), dated October 31, 1968. Translation of a report "On Security Situation and Mission (from July 5 to October 3, 1968)," prepared by elements in Gia Lai Province, B-3 Front, on October 13, 1968. Captured by the 477th RF Company, RVNAF II CTZ, on October 18, 1968.

14. Doc. Log No. 10-1004-68 (Confidential), dated November 10, 1968 (emphasis added). Translation of a "Resolution" (activity plan) prepared at the Dai Loc District Party Committee Conference, Quang Da Province, which was held from May 24 to May 28, 1968. The Resolution was dated May 25, 1968, and was classified Secret. Captured by the 1st USMC Division on September 14, 1968.

15. Doc. Log No. 01-2311-69 (Confidential), dated January 31, 1969 (emphasis added). Translation of a "Plan for Political Struggle

and Armed Uprising. . . ," dated December 22, 1968, and attributed to the Political Struggle Section of the Binh Dinh Province Party Committee. Captured by the Capital ROK Infantry Division on January 4, 1969.

16. Doc. Log No. 05-1385-68 (Confidential), summarized in MACJ2 Bulletin No. 12,150, dated May 7, 1968 (emphasis added). Summary of an activity plan of an unidentified Village Security Section for the period of April 15 to June 30, 1968. Captured by the 7/1 Cavalry Squadron, II FFV, on April 24, 1968.

17. Doc. Log No. 10-2095-68 (Confidential), dated October 31, 1968 (emphasis added). Translation of a "Directive on Political Tasks for Winter 1968," dated October 5, 1968, and attributed to the Political Section, Gia Lai Province Unit, B-3 Front. Captured by RF, 24th STZ, RVNAF II CTZ, between October 18 and 20, 1968. Similar statements may be found in numerous other captured documents, such as Doc. Log No. 01-1999-68 (Confidential), summarized in MACJ2 Bulletin No. 9057, dated January 20, 1968, and Doc. Log No. 05-1947-68 (Confidential), summarized in MACJ2 Bulletin No. 12,415, dated May 15, 1968.

18. Examples appear in Doc. Log No. 02-2050-68 (Confidential), summarized in MACJ2 Bulletin No. 9769, dated February 25, 1968, and Doc. Log No. 04-3157-68 (Confidential), summarized in MACJ2 Bulletin No. 11,901, dated April 30, 1968.

19. Doc. Log No. 11-1520-68 (Confidential), dated December 26, 1968. Translation of a plan prepared by an unidentified enemy unit concerning military and political operations against Allied targets in Ben Tre Province in 1968. Captured by 5th U.S. SFGA on November 6, 1968.

20. Doc. Log No. 01-2268-69 (Confidential), dated February 17, 1969. Translation of a "Directive" dated October 4, 1968, believed to have been issued by the Current Affairs Committee, COSVN, concerning the intelligence activities of the GVN's "Phuong Hoang" (Phoenix) program and the measures necessary to counter that organization. Captured by the C/K/RAR, lst ATF, on January 19, 1969.

21. Doc. Log No. 11-1520-68 (see n. 19).

22. Doc. Log No. 02-1076-69 (Confidential), dated February 20, 1969. Translation of a Secret letter, dated October 24, 1968, believed to have been prepared by an agency of Subregion 2 and addressed to the Security Sections of Precinct 6 (Saigon) and five other districts in surrounding areas of Subregion 2. Captured by the 25th U.S. Infantry Division on January 26, 1969.

23. Examples were found in the following: Doc. Log No. 01-3001-67 (Confidential), dated December 12, 1967; Doc. Log No. 05-2047-67 (Confidential), dated February 12, 1968; Doc. Log No. 12-1739-67 (Confidential), dated December 29, 1967; Doc. Log No. 03-1120-68 (Confidential), summarized in MACJ2 Bulletin No. 9986, dated March 2, 1968; Doc. Log No. 04-1228-68 (Confidential), dated May 16, 1968; and Doc. Log No. 10-1399-68 (Confidential), dated October 27, 1968.

24. Doc. Log No. 11-1020-68 (Confidential), dated January 15, 1969. Translation of a directive pertaining to a six-month propaganda campaign (from October 1968 to March 1969), believed to have been issued by an agency of Ben Tre Province on October 17, 1968. Captured by the 9th U.S. Infantry Division on October 29, 1968.

25. Doc. Log No. 10-2137-68 (Confidential), dated November 17, 1968. Translation of a directive dated September 23, 1968, entitled "Policies, Subjects and Requirements of Propaganda Mission (from October 1968 to March 1969)" and attributed to the Political Staff of Military Region VII. Captured by the 1st RAR Battalion, 1st ATF, on October 8, 1968.

26. Doc. Log No. 04-2435-68 (Confidential), dated May 31, 1968. Translation of a letter which sets forth security procedures for the Security Section of an unidentified province in line with COSVN and Military Region resolutions. Captured by the C/3/RAR, 1st ATF, on March 30, 1968.

27. Doc. Log No. 12-0503-67 (Confidential), dated January 23, 1968. Translation of a propaganda leaflet addressed to "all people of the province," issued by the Saigon-Gia Dinh Region National Front for Liberation Committee in late 1967. Captured by the 5th ARVN Ranger Group, Gia Dinh Sector, on December 8 or 9, 1967.

28. Doc. Log No. 06-1939-69 (see n.7).

29. "Liberation Medals" are awarded to units or individuals who show outstanding courage in liquidating "tyrants." The Special Action element of the Quang Da City Unit, for example, was awarded a Third Class Liberation Medal for the high fighting spirit and courage displayed in killing three "tyrants" in Nhan Bien hamlet on August 3, 1967. Doc. Log No. 10-1915-68 (Confidential), summarized in MACJ2 Bulletin No. 17,356, dated October 19, 1968. Captured by the 1st U.S. Air Cavalry Division.

30. An example is Doc. Log No. 01-1142-69 (Confidential), summarized in MACJ2 Bulletin No. 19,243, dated January 3, 1969,

which summarizes notes taken at a political reorientation training course held in Military Region V during December 1968. Captured by the Americal Division on December 18, 1968.

31. Doc. Log No. 02-1922-68 (Confidential), dated February 29, 1968. Translation of minutes concerning a meeting of the Military Affairs Party Committee, Area 3, which reviewed the combat achievements of Area 3 during the Tet Offensive. Captured by CMD, RVNAF III CTZ, on February 12, 1968.

32. Doc. Log No. 09-2102-68 (Confidential), dated October 15, 1968. Translation of a directive dated August 5, 1968, concerning "Political Struggle and Armed Uprising," believed to have been issued by the Current Affairs Committee of a district in Binh Dinh Province. Captured by the 5th U.S. SFGA on September 11, 1968.

33. Doc. Log No. 01-1291-69 (Confidential), dated January 28, 1969. Translation of a letter dated December 14, 1968, concerning measures which should be introduced to counter GVN pacification activities in certain villages, believed to be in Hoa Vang District, Quang Da Province. Captured by PLC, FMF, on December 18, 1968.

34. Doc. Log No. 10-2110-68 (Confidential), dated October 31, 1968. Translation of a directive dated September 24, 1968, concerning "Political Struggle Plan for Crop Protection," issued by elements of Gia Lai Province, B-3 Front. Captured by RF, 24th STZ, RVNAF II CTZ, between October 18 and 20, 1968.

35. Doc. Log No. 03-1251-69 (Confidential), presented in MACJ2 Bulletin No. 20,918, dated March 11, 1969. Translation of an "Order" dated February 25, 1969, issued by the Command Committee, Armed Forces of the Saigon-Gia Dinh Area, South Vietnam Liberation Army. Captured by the 25th U.S. Infantry Division on March 6, 1969.

36. Doc. Log No. 03-5010-69 (Confidential), summarized in MACJ2 Bulletin No. 15, dated March 6, 1969, concerning a directive issued by the Administrative Staff, Binh Tan District Party Committee, Subregion 2, on January 20, 1969. Captured by the 82d U.S. Airborne Division on February 14, 1969.

37. Doc. Log No. 12-2004-68 (Confidential), summarized in MACJ2 Bulletin No. 18,906, dated December 21, 1968. Summary of a circular dated September 23, 1968, and attributed to the Current Affairs Committee, Subregion 1, concerning measures to counter the GVN's ID-card program. Captured by the 25th U.S. Infantry Division on December 18, 1968.

38. Doc. Log No. 06-1096-68 (Confidential), dated July 24,

1968. Translation of a list of "Crimes Caused by Imperialists and Feudalists" in an unidentified area. Captured by the 196th Light Infantry Brigade, Americal Division, on April 5, 1968.

39. Doc. Log No. 01-2708-69 (Confidential), summarized in MACJ2 Bulletin No. 20,165, dated January 29, 1969. Letter dated January 25, 1969, concerning security activities; attributed to a cadre of Subregion 1. Captured by the 25th U.S. Infantry Division on January 26, 1969.

40. Doc. Log No. 10-1570-68 (Confidential), dated November 2, 1968. Translation of a "Report" on the "Enemy Situation in July 1968," prepared by the Military Staff, South Vietnam Liberation Army, Subregion 4, on July 31, 1968. Captured by the C/4/RAR Battalion, lst ATF, on September 18, 1968.

41. Doc. Log No. 09-1544-68 (Confidential), dated September 16, 1968. Translation of a Secret "Circular on Political and Ideological Indoctrination Against Desertion and Surrender," believed to have been issued by the Dong Nai Regiment, Subregion 5, on August 9, 1968. Captured by the 1st U.S. Infantry Division on September 2, 1968.

42. Doc. Log No. 07-1030-66 (Confidential), summarized in MACJ2 Bulletin No. 629, dated July 7, 1966. Summary of a Secret memorandum (concerning the detection and prevention of desertion and betrayal) produced by the Political Staff of the Phuoc Long Province Unit on May 6, 1966. Captured by the 101st Airborne Division on May 15, 1966.

43. This also applies in the case of Viet Cong personnel who are captured by the GVN and who are recruited as intelligence agents prior to being released. For example, Doc. Log No. 02-5268-69 (Confidential), summarized in MACJ2 Bulletin No. 7, dated February 20, 1969. Summary of a circular dated April 14, 1968, which authorizes local agencies to assassinate Viet Cong personnel who have been recruited as intelligence agents while prisoners of war. Captured by the lst U.S. Cavalry Division (Airmobile) on February 11, 1969.

44. For example, Doc. Log No. 03-1320-68 (Confidential), summarized in MACJ2 Bulletin No. 10,090, dated March 6, 1968. Summary of a "military proselytizing plan for 1967 and 1968," attributed to the Military Proselytizing Section of Go Mon District, Subregion 1. Captured by the 25th U.S. Infantry Division on March 2, 1968.

45. Doc. Log No. 04-1026-66 (Confidential), dated April 26,

1966. Translation of a Top Secret "Security Plan for 1966," dated March 15, 1966, which covers various security activities in Kontum Province. Captured by USSF Det 242 on March 23, 1966.

46. Doc. Log No. 12-2719-67 (Confidential), summarized in MACJ2 Bulletin No. 8659, dated December 27, 1967. Summary of a directive dated October 29, 1967, concerning various missions to be performed by village Party Committees in an unspecified area of Military Region V. Captured by the 4th U.S. Infantry Division on December 7, 1967.

47. Doc. Log No. 01-1428-69 (Confidential), dated February 6, 1969. Translation of a "Situation Report" covering the period November 29 to December 10, 1968, prepared by the Current Affairs Committee, Hai Lang District, Quang Tri Province. The report is dated December 13, 1968. Captured by the 3rd USMC Division, FMF, on December 23, 1968.

48. Doc. Log No. 05-2503-67 (Confidential), dated November 14, 1967. Extract translation of situation report on Tay Ninh Province for the period February 25 to March 25, 1967, dated April 15, 1967, prepared by the Current Affairs Committee, Tay Ninh Province. Captured by the 25th U.S. Infantry Division on May 7, 1967.

49. Doc. Log No. 01-3347-67 (Confidential), dated January 28, 1968. Translation of a Top Secret directive concerning security maintenance missions and guidelines for subordinate echelons, issued by the Current Affairs Section of COSVN in November 1966. Attached to this document was a second Top Secret directive, issued by the Current Affairs Section of Military Region IV on December 11, 1966, and relating to the implementation of the COSVN directive [cited above]. Captured by the 25th U.S. Infantry Division on January 17, 1967.

50. Doc. Log No. 02-1603-69 (Confidential), dated March 30, 1969. Translation of a directive dated November 5, 1968 (concerning the intensification of activities designed to "frustrate" the GVN's "urgent pacification plan"), attributed to the My Tho City HQ, My Tho Province, Military Region II. Captured by the 9th U.S. Infantry Division on February 2, 1969.

51. Doc. Log No. 01-1581-69 (Confidential), summarized in MACJ2 Bulletin No. 19,504, dated January 10, 1969. Summary of a directive dated December 12, 1968, setting forth instructions for the disruption of the GVN's accelerated pacification plan in Subregion 5. Issued by the Deputy Commander, HQ Subregion 5. Captured by the 11th U.S. Armored Cavalry Regiment on January 4, 1969.

52. Doc. Log No. 02-1787-69 (Confidential), dated March 6, 1969. Translation of a letter dated November 26, 1968, by an unidentified enemy agency which provides detailed information on the "Phuong Hoang" organization (including its mission and activities) and urges appropriate countermeasures. Captured by CTU 194.9.5., U.S. Navy, on February 16, 1969.

53. Doc. Log No. 01-2268-69 (see n. 20).

54. Doc. Log No. 07-1770-67 (see n. 3).

55. Doc. Log No. 01-3347-67 (see n. 49).

56. Doc. Log No. 07-1092-66 (Confidential), summarized in MACJ2 Bulletin No. 648, dated July 12, 1966. Summary of a Secret circular dated April 20, 1965, outlining the prerogatives and responsibilites of various Party echelons in the arrest, detention, and execution of persons in "liberated" and disputed areas. This circular is believed to have been issued by the Security Section of Military Region V. Captured by the 1st U.S. Air Cavalry Division on May 6, 1966.

57. Doc. Log No. 07-1770-67 (see n. 3).

58. For example, Doc. Log No. 07-1123-66 (Confidential), summarized in MACJ2 Bulletin No. 657, dated July 12, 1966; Doc. Log No. 07-1018-66 (Confidential), summarized in MACJ2 Bulletin No. 624, dated July 6, 1966; Doc. Log No. 12-2487-67 (Confidential), summarized in MACJ2 Bulletin No. 8603, dated December 22, 1967; and Doc. Log No. 06-3191-67 (Confidential), dated December 23, 1967.

59. For example, Doc. Log No. 04-1826-68 (Confidential), summarized in MACJ2 Bulletin No. 11,245, dated April 10, 1968; Doc. Log No. 05-1837-68 (Confidential), summarized in MACJ2 Bulletin No. 12,363, dated May 14, 1968; and Doc. Log No. 12-1072-67 (Confidential), summarized in MACJ2 Bulletin No. 8242, dated December 1, 1967.

60. One illustration of this policy was found in a cadre's notebook containing lessons on the tactics to be employed during an attack on Quang Tri City in January 1968. According to the notebook, the destruction of churches in Quang Tri City and terrorist actions against Catholics were prohibited. In addition, attacking units were instructed to take care of Catholic priests and motivate them to demand peace and freedom of faith as well as the withdrawal of U.S. forces from Vietnam. Doc. Log No. 07-1093-68 (Confidential), summarized in MACJ2 Bulletin No. 13,906, dated July 2, 1968. Captured by the 1st U.S. Air Cavalry Division.

61. Doc. Log No. 11-1474-67 (Confidential), dated March 28, 1968. Translation of a report dated July 1, 1967 (entitled "Progress and Shortcomings of the Troops and Enemy Proselyting Activities Conducted by Armed and Paramilitary Forces Since the Beginning of 1967"), issued by an agency of Phu Yen Province, Military Region V. Captured by the 173rd U.S. Airborne Brigade on October 25, 1967.

62. Doc. Log No. 04-1340-68 (Confidential), summarized in MACJ2 Bulletin No. 11,023, dated April 5, 1968. Summary of a notebook containing entries dated between August 21, 1967, and January 1968, believed to have belonged to a cadre of the 81st Battalion. Captured by the Americal Division on January 20, 1968.

63. General W. C. Westmoreland, USA, "Report on Operations in South Vietnam, January 1964-1968," in *Report on the War in Vietnam*, U.S. Government Printing Office, Washington, D.C., p. 158.

64. Doc. Log No. 02-1290-68, summarized in MACJ2 Bulletin No. 9388, dated February 9, 1968. Summary of a directive (in letter form) dated November 1, 1967, attributed to the Secretary of the Ban Me Thuot Province Party Committee which provided guidelines to subordinate echelons for the implementation of the forthcoming offensive and uprising order. Captured in Pleiku City on January 30, 1968.

65. Doc. Log No. 03-2623-68 (Confidential), dated May 1, 1968. Translation of a "Plan for Attacking and Securing District Seats in the Subregion" during the Tet Offensive, prepared by the Military Affairs Committee, Subregion 1, on January 29, 1968. Captured by the 1st U.S. Infantry Division on March 25, 1968.

66. Doc. Log No. 05-2817-68 (Confidential), summarized in MACJ2 Bulletin No. 12,882, dated May 30, 1968. Summary of a "Resolution" passed by the Current Affairs Committee of the Region V Party Committee at a meeting held on February 23, 1968. Captured by the 4th U.S. Infantry Division on May 20, 1968.

67. Doc. Log No. 02-1114-68 (Confidential), dated February 8, 1968. Translation of an undated "Attack Order" addressed to "All Cadres and Men of the Liberation Army," issued by the Presidium of the Central Committee, National Front for the Liberation of South Vietnam. Captured by the 25th U.S. Infantry Division on February 3, 1968.

68. Doc. Log No. 02-1060-69 (Confidential), summarized in MACJ2 Bulletin No. 20,272, dated February 2, 1969. Summary of a Top Secret directive dated February 11, 1968 (providing guidance

for the elimination of "reactionaries"), which is believed to have been issued by the Current Affairs Committee of Subregion 1. Captured by the 25th U.S. Infantry Division on January 26, 1969.

69. Doc. Log No. 05-2068-68 (Confidential), dated June 19, 1968 (emphasis added). Translation of an undated training document pertaining to the implementation of the 6th COSVN Resolution by all levels of the Party. The document was entitled "Requirement and Purpose of the Study of the Sixth Resolution of Nam Truong" and was presumably prepared at a high level. Captured by the lst U.S. Infantry Division on May 6, 1968.

70. Doc. Log No. 02-2083-68 (Confidential), dated February 28, 1968 (emphasis added). Translation of an activity plan which provides an assessment of the progress achieved during the first seven days of the Tet Offensive and outlines plans for the continuation of that offensive. The document was entitled "Capitalize on Our Victories To Dash Forward and Continuously Attack the Enemy, with a Strong Determination To Gain Final Victory," and was prepared on February 5, 1968, at an otherwise unspecified Current Affairs Party Committee meeting. (The contents of the document would suggest that the issuing agency may have been the Current Affairs Committee of COSVN.) Captured by the 25th U.S. Infantry Division on February 24, 1968.

71. Doc. Log No. 04-2670-68 (Confidential), summarized in MACJ2 Bulletin No. 11,665, dated April 22, 1968. Summary of an undated "appeal" published by the Saigon-Gia Dinh United Liberation Youth Association and addressed to the people and students of the Saigon-Gia Dinh area. Captured by the combined MP Tm, CMD, RVNAF III CTZ, on April 21, 1968.

72. For example, Doc. Log No. 05-2819-68 (Confidential), summarized in MACJ2 Bulletin No. 12,883, dated May 30, 1968. Summary of a training document dated May 5, 1968, published by the Propaganda-Training Section of Subregion 1 as a training lesson for cadres and Party members on how to master the main problems in the motivation of the populace to revolt. Captured by the lst U.S. Infantry Division on May 21, 1968.

73. For example, Doc. Log No. 01-2766-69 (Confidential), summarized in MACJ2 Bulletin No. 20,197, dated January 30, 1969, and Doc. Log No. 01-2818-69 (Confidential), summarized in MACJ2 Bulletin No. 20,230, dated January 31, 1969.

74. Doc. Log No. 11-1771-68 (Confidential), summarized in MACJ2 Bulletin No. 18,033, dated November 19, 1968. Summary of

a "Recapitulation Report" dated October 30, 1968, which reviews the political struggle movement in Binh Dinh Province during the months prior to October 20, 1968, and provides lessons for future political struggles. Captured by the Capital ROK Infantry Division on November 6, 1968.

75. Doc. Log No. 01-2762-69 (Confidential), summarized in MACJ2 Bulletin No. 20,195, dated January 30, 1969. Summary of a directive dated November 10, 1968, which provides guidance to province units concerning the tasks of guerrilla and self-defense units during a forthcoming campaign. This directive is attributed to the Political Department, Headquarters, Military Region V. Captured by the Capital ROK Infantry Division on January 4, 1969.

76. Doc. Log No. 01-2773-69 (Confidential), summarized in MACJ2 Bulletin No. 20,203, dated January 30, 1969. Summary of a Top Secret plan dated December 12, 1968, attributed to an agency of the Binh Dinh Province Unit, Military Region V, which provides guidance on military proselytizing activities in a forthcoming campaign. Captured by the Capital ROK Infantry Division on January 4, 1969.

77. Doc. Log No. 10-1003-68 (Confidential), dated November 23, 1968. Translation of directive (in draft form) dated June 19, 1968, concerning the "Strategy and Tactics of Launching Permanent and Continuous Attacks Against the Enemy During Military Campaigns and Operations." This directive is believed to have been prepared by the Tri-Thien-Hue Military Region. Captured by the 196th Light Infantry Brigade, Americal Division, on September 9, 1968.

78. Doc. Log No. 11-1520-68 (see n. 19).

79. Doc. Log No. 07-3297-68 (Confidential), summarized in MACJ2 Bulletin No. 15,030, dated July 31, 1968. Summary of an undated attack plan prepared by an agency in the Quang Da Special Zone, with details for an attack to be launched against an unspecified city. Captured by the 11th Light Infantry Brigade, Americal Division, on July 23, 1968.

80. Doc. Log No. 08-1045-68 (Confidential), dated August 15, 1968. Translation of a notebook dated June 30, 1968, concerning the activities of district agencies in Thua Thien Province. Captured by the 1st USMC Division, III MAF, on July 21, 1968.

81. Doc. Log No. 02-5567-69 (Confidential), summarized in MACJ2 Bulletin No. 16, dated March 6, 1969. Summary of letter dated July 1968, and containing instructions on the conduct of security activities in Ben Tre City and its outskirts during a

forthcoming phase of hostilities. This letter is attributed to the Security Section, Ben Tre Province Unit, Military Region II. Captured by the 9th U.S. Infantry Division in February 1969.

82. Doc. Log No. 01-2117-69 (Confidential), dated February 20, 1969. Translation of an "Activity Plan" (classified Absolute Secret) adopted by the Tuy An District Unit, Phu Yen Province, at the Guerrilla Warfare Congress held on November 2, 1968. Captured by RF/PF, Tuy An District, Phu Yen Province, RVNAF II CTZ, on December 31, 1968.

83. Doc. Log No. 03-2774-68 (Confidential), dated May 3, 1968. Translation of a "Plan of Military Activity of the Go Mon [District Unit] for December 1967 and January 1968" prepared by the Go Mon District Military Affairs Committee, Subregion 1, on December 18, 1967. Captured by the 1st U.S. Infantry Division on March 25, 1968.

84. Doc. Log No. 12-1886-67 (Confidential), dated January 26, 1968. Translation of "Specific Military Plans for the Winter and Spring [campaign] of 1967-68 of the Chau Duc [District Unit]," dated October 30, 1967, and prepared by the Command Committee, Chau Duc District Unit, Ba Bien Province. Captured by the D/7 RAR, lst ATF, on November 27, 1967.

85. Doc. Log No. 08-2515-68 (Confidential), summarized in MACJ2 Bulletin No. 15,848, dated August 26, 1968. Summary of a letter dated August 3, 1968, attributed to an element of the Binh Dinh Province Party Committee, Military Region V, and addressed to subordinate villages of that province. Captured by the Capital ROK Infantry Division on August 4, 1968.

86. For example, Doc. Log No. 12-2041-68 (Confidential), summarized in MACJ2 Bulletin No. 18,931, dated December 22, 1968. Summary of a Top Secret order dated December 1, 1968 (attributed to the Kien Phong Province Party Current Affairs Committee, Military Region II), which directs subordinate district units to kill from ten to twenty GVN administrative personnel in various villages. Captured by the 44th SZ, RVNAF IV CTZ, on December 9, 1968.

Chapter 3
The Blacklists

1. Doc. Log No. 07-1770-67 (see Chap. 2, n. 3).
2. *Ibid.*

---

3. *Ibid.*

4. Doc. Log No. 05-1220-67 (Confidential), dated May 30, 1967. Translation of a Secret directive (concerning the "organization and stepping up of intelligence and security activities in cities and towns") which is attributed to either the Security Section of COSVN or Military Region I. The document is undated, but appears from the text to have been written in 1964. Captured by the 1st U.S. Infantry Division on April 27, 1967.

5. Doc. Log No. 01-2624-67 (Confidential), dated February 11, 1967 (emphasis added). Translation of a Top Secret directive (concerning "the duties, organization and working methods of [the] security apparatus at the district, city and township echelons") issued by the Current Affairs Committee of an unspecified province on August 1, 1966. Captured by the 1st U.S. Infantry Division on January 12, 1967.

6. Doc. Log No. 01-1606-68 (Confidential), dated January 18, 1968. Translation of a directive providing instructions for military and political activities in Phu Cuong City and its vicinity for the period from October 1967 to October 1968. The document, published by an unidentified unit in Binh Duong Province, was dated July 30, 1967. Captured by the 794th RF Co., Binh Duong Sector, RVNAF III CTZ, on January 8, 1968.

7. Doc. Log No. 04-1860-68 (Confidential), summarized in MACJ2 Bulletin No. 11,261, dated April 11, 1968. Summary of a Top Secret directive dated August 13, 1967, and attributed to an element of the 5th NVA Division. Captured by the 9th ROK Infantry Division on February 13, 1968.

8. Doc. Log No. 01-2220-68 (Confidential), summarized in MACJ2 Bulletin No. 9155, dated January 24, 1968. Summary of a directive dated November 12, 1967 (concerning plans for the 1967-68 Winter-Spring campaign), attributed to the Current Affairs Committee, Long Thanh District Party Committee, Ba Bien Province. Captured by the 9th U.S. Infantry Division on January 22, 1968.

9. Doc. Log No. 08-2515-68 (see Chap. 2, n. 85).

10. Doc. Log No. 07-1770-67 (see Chap. 2, n. 3).

11. Doc. Log No. 08-1208-66 (Confidential), summarized in MACJ2 Bulletin No. 802, dated August 11, 1966. Summary of a directive issued by the Security Section of Thua Thien Province on August 24, 1965, which outlined security missions for subordinate echelons during the remainder of 1965. Captured by the 3rd MAF on July 8, 1966.

12. Doc. Log No. 04-1026-66 (see Chap. 2, n. 45).

13. Doc. Log No. 12-2319-68 (Confidential), summarized in MACJ2 Bulletin No. 19,088, dated December 29, 1968. Summary of a plan, dated October 22, 1968, concerning the promotion of a mass uprising in a village of Hoa Vang District, Quang Da Special Zone. Captured by the lst USMC Division between 3 and 6 December 1968.

14. Doc. Log No. 02-2273-68 (Confidential), summarized in MACJ2 Bulletin No. 9896, dated February 28, 1968. Summary of a letter, dated December 20, 1967, attributed to elements in Dien Ban District, Quang Da Province. Captured by the lst USMC Division, between February 8 and 9, 1968.

15. For example, Doc. Log No. 05-1286-67 (Confidential), dated June 7, 1967. Translation of a directive dated March 4, 1966, prepared by the Security Section of Military Region I, concerning the organization and missions of the Espionage Subsection (B 3) in MR I. Captured by the 1st U.S. Infantry Division on April 27, 1967.

16. Doc. Log No. 07-2928-68 (Confidential), summarized in MACJ2 Bulletin No. 14,880, dated July 28, 1968. Summary of a notebook (with entries dated between March 8 and May 10, 1968) maintained by an intelligence cell leader in Hue City. Captured by the 101st Air Cavalry Division on July 17, 1968.

17. Doc. Log No. 09-1415-68 (Confidential), summarized in MACJ2 Bulletin No. 16,306, dated September 7, 1968. Summary of personal papers and personnel rosters (including names and biographic data on 70 RVNAF soldiers and other GVN personnel) maintained by a Viet Cong informer in Da Nang City. Acquired by the 5th CIT, III US MAF, on August 19, 1968.

18. Doc. Log No. 06-1267-68 (Confidential), summarized in MACJ2 Bulletin No. 13,061, dated June 5, 1968. Translation of a recorded conversation between two Viet Cong agents in Kien Hoa Province. Acquired by the 9th U.S. Infantry Division on May 14, 1968.

19. Doc. Log No. 03-2678-68 (Confidential), summarized in MACJ2 Bulletin No. 10,756, dated March 28, 1968. Summary of a Top Secret report dated February 20, 1968, and prepared by the Political Staff of Subregion 1. Captured by the lst U.S. Infantry Division on March 25, 1968.

20. Doc. Log No. 05-1286-67 (see n. 15).

21. Doc. Log No. 02-1354-68 (Confidential), summarized in MACJ2 Bulletin No. 9417, dated February 10, 1968. Summary of a Secret directive (in letter form) addressed to district security cadres in Subregion 1, which outlined the mission of limiting the antirevolu-

tionary activities of various government "targets." Captured by the 25th U.S. Infantry Division on February 5, 1968.

22. For example, Doc. Log No. 07-2289-68 (Confidential), summarized in MACJ2 Bulletin No. 14,535, dated July 19, 1968.

23. Doc. Log No. 05-1286-67 (see n. 15).

24. Doc. Log No. 06-1909-68 (Confidential), dated August 19, 1968. Translation of a Top Secret list entitled "Location of a Number of Objectives in Hue City," believed to have been prepared by an agency of the Hue City Unit. This list was attached to another document (entitled "Report on the Meeting of the City Unit Civil Affairs Committee") prepared by the Hue City Unit. Captured by the lst U.S. Air Cavalry Division on June 12, 1968.

25. Three captured notebooks, with entries dated between February and April 1968, contained "blacklists" of GVN officials, RVNAF personnel, and Vietnamese employees working for the U.S. Government in Hue City and its outskirts. Doc. Log No. 06-2581-68 (Confidential), summarized in MACJ2 Bulletin No. 13,766, dated June 28, 1968. Captured by PRU, Thua Thien Sector, RVNAF I CTZ.

26. Doc. Log No. 04-2527-68 (Confidential), summarized in MACJ2 Bulletin No. 11,587, dated April 19, 1968. "Blacklists" found in two notebooks maintained by security cadres in Cam Lo and Trieu Phong Districts, Quang Tri Province. Captured by the 3rd USMC Division on March 29, 1968.

27. Doc. Log No. 05-2572-68 (Confidential) summarized in MACJ2 Bulletin No. 12,755, dated May 26, 1968. Captured by the 199th U.S. Light Infantry Brigade on May 20, 1968.

28. Doc. Log No. 06-1569-68 (Confidential), summarized in MACJ2 Bulletin No. 13,227, dated June 11, 1968. Captured by the 25th U.S. Infantry Division on June 8, 1968.

29. *Ibid.*

30. Doc. Log No. 08-1502-66 (Confidential), summarized in MACJ2 Bulletin No. 854, dated August 20, 1966. Summary of a notebook, believed to have been maintained by the Chief of the Huong Thuy District Security Subsection, containing several rosters of GVN administrative personnel marked down for execution. Captured by a unit of the III MAF on July 9, 1966.

31. Doc. Log No. 06-2581-68 (see n. 25).

32. Doc. Log No. 07-2208-68 (Confidential), summarized in MACJ2 Bulletin No. 14,495, dated July 18, 1968. Summary of a

notebook, with entries dated between March 1966 and October 1967, maintained by an unidentified cadre in Duc Duc District, Quang Nam Province. The notebook contained several rosters listing the names of more than 50 GVN intelligence agents operating in Duc Duc District. Captured by the 11th Infantry Brigade, Americal Division, on April 10, 1968.

33. Doc. Log No. 05-1502-66 (Confidential), dated May 30, 1966. Translation of a November 1965 report prepared by an unidentified Security Service agency on eleven persons selected by the GVN to attend an intelligence course at Cay Mai School (Cholon). Captured by the 21st Infantry Division on May 14, 1966.

34. Doc. Log No. 01-1229-68 (Confidential), summarized in MACJ2 Bulletin No. 8797, dated January 5, 1968. Captured by the 173rd U.S. Airborne Brigade on December 20, 1967.

35. Doc. Log No.04-2435-68 (see Chap. 2, n. 26).

36. Doc. Log No. 12-1300-67 (Confidential), summarized in MACJ2 Bulletin No. 8298, dated December 5, 1967. Summary of a Secret directive dated October 15, 1967, and attributed to the Security Section of the Go Dau District Unit, Tay Ninh Province. Captured by the 25th U.S. Infantry Division on November 29, 1967.

37. Doc. Log No. 03-2053-68 (Confidential), summarized in MACJ2 Bulletin No. 10,473, dated March 19, 1968. Summary of a notebook with entries dated from December 14, 1965, to January 27, 1968, which had been maintained by an unidentified security cadre of Thanh Tuyen Village, Go Mon District, Subregion 1. Captured by the 25th U.S. Infantry Division.

38. Doc. Log No. 04-2696-68 (Confidential), dated May 27, 1968. Translation of a "Plan for the Activities of the 1967-1968 Winter-Spring Phase," believed to have been prepared by an agency of Lai Thieu District, Thu Dau Mot Province. Captured by the Lai Thieu Subsector, Binh Duong Sector, RVNAF III CTZ, on April 5, 1968.

39. Doc. Log No. 04-3053-68 (Confidential), summarized in MACJ2 Bulletin No. 11,847, dated April 28, 1968. Captured by the Duc Phong Special Forces, RVNAF III CTZ, on April 12, 1968.

40. Doc. Log No. 07-3294-68 (Confidential), summarized in MACJ2 Bulletin No. 15,029, dated July 31, 1968. Summary of a notebook believed to have been maintained by a cadre of the Trang Bang District Security Section, Subregion 1. Captured by the 101st U.S. Air Cavalry Division on July 28, 1968.

41. Doc. Log No. 03-1637-68 (Confidential), summarized in MACJ2 Bulletin No. 10,262, dated March 11, 1968. Captured by the 25th U.S. Infantry Division on March 1, 1968.

42. Doc. Log No. 01-2152-67 (Confidential), dated April 27, 1967. Translation of a report of an "Investigation on the Situation in Trung An 2 Village" prepared by the Security Section of that village on November 20, 1966. Captured by the 25th U.S. Infantry Division on January 9, 1967.

43. Doc. Log No. 06-1338-66 (Confidential), summarized in MACJ2 Bulletin No. 576, dated June 25, 1966. Summary of the Annual Report for 1965 by Ca Mau Province. Captured by the 21st RVNAF Infantry Division on May 14, 1966.

44. Doc. Log No. 06-1216-66 (Confidential), summarized in MACJ2 Bulletin No. 535, dated June 16, 1966. Summary of the February 1966 Security Report by the Security Section of Military Region III. Captured by the 21st RVNAF Infantry Division on May 14, 1966.

45. Doc. Log No. 02-1064-69 (Confidential), summarized in MACJ2 Bulletin No. 20,274, dated February 2, 1969. Summary of a report attributed to the Security Section of the Trang Bang District Unit, Subregion 1. Captured by the 25th U.S. Infantry Division on January 26, 1969.

46. Doc. Log No. 06-1939-69, emphasis added (see Chap. 2, n. 7).

Chapter 4
The Forms of Repression

1. United States Mission in Vietnam, "North Vietnam's Role in the South," in *Viet-Nam Documents and Research Notes*, Document Nos. 36-37, June 1968, p. 22.

2. Supplement No. 2 to United States Mission pamphlet "A Study—Viet Cong Use of Terror," March 1967.

3. Many thousands more were wounded in terrorist activity, including attempts at assassination. According to the TIRS data, a total of 31,364 persons were wounded in terrorist incidents during 1968 and 1969 alone. Among these victims were 326 government officials and 2,622 government employees.

4. According to the TIRS data, village and hamlet officials accounted for 960 of the 996 government officials assassinated or abducted during 1968 and 1969.

5. National Police personnel and Rural Development cadres accounted for 1,027 of the 1,210 government employees whom the TIRS listed as killed or abducted in 1968 and 1969.

6. In their reporting, local Viet Cong units usually claim that

such "terrorist" attacks are directed against legitimate targets. For example, the Cu Chi Armed Reconnaissance Unit reported on December 21, 1968, that two of its agents, riding a Honda motorbike, threw four grenades into a coffee shop in Cu Chi District, killing fourteen GVN policemen and wounding ten others (including three civilians). One of the terrorists was killed while attempting to escape. Both the deceased and the surviving agent were awarded the Liberation Military Exploit Medal. Doc. Log No. 01-2705-69 (Confidential), summarized in MACJ2 Bulletin No. 20,163, dated January 29, 1969. Captured by the 25th U.S. Infantry Division on January 26, 1969.

7. One example of the types of persons abducted by the Communists is provided in a report dated September 20, 1968, attributed to the Security Section, Trang Bang District, Subregion 1. According to this report, an armed security unit kidnapped 24 persons during an attack on a village in Trang Bang District, including military intelligence agents, "Chieu Hoi" personnel, Home Guard and Self-Defense personnel, and some suspects. Doc. Log No. 01-2797-69 (Confidential), summarized in MACJ2 Bulletin No. 20,217, dated January 31, 1969. Captured by the 25th U.S. Infantry Division on January 26, 1969.

8. Although the captured documents contain few specific reports of assassinations of relatives and dependents of government persons, there are some. One 1968 document, for example, reported the murder of the wives of two GVN persons in Binh Tan District; another 1968 report revealed the killing of the dependents of two RVNAF soldiers in Duc Hoa District. Doc. Log No. 02-1922-68 (see Chap. 2, n. 31) and Doc. Log No. 05-1480-68 (Confidential), summarized in MACJ2 Bulletin No. 12,197, dated May 8, 1968.

9. Doc. Log No. 03-2497-68 (Confidential), dated March 29, 1968. Translation of an after-action report dated February 27, 1968, on the Tet Offensive in Saigon; attributed to the Security Section of the Saigon-Cholon-Gia Dinh Military Region. Captured by the 199th U.S. Light Infantry Brigade on March 21, 1968.

10. *Ibid.*

11. *Ibid.*

12. General W. C. Westmoreland, USA, "Report on Operations in South Vietnam, January 1964-1968" (see Chap. 2, n. 63), pp. 159-160.

13. Doc. Log No. 02-2198-68 (Confidential), summarized in MACJ2 Bulletin No. 9853, dated February 27, 1968. Summary of a

notebook recording minutes of a plenary session of a Party
Committee meeting held in January 1968; believed to have been
maintained by a cadre of the 29th Regiment, 325C NVA Division.
Captured by the 101st U.S. Airborne Division on February 22 or 23,
1968.

14. Doc. Log No. 05-1131-68 (Confidential), dated May 29,
1968. Translation of an undated report classified Absolute Secret
entitled "Information on the Victory of Our Armed Forces in Hue
from 31 January to 23 March 1968." Captured by the 1st U.S. Air
Cavalry Division on April 25, 1968. Doc. Log No. 02-5276-69
(Confidential), dated May 8, 1969. Translation of a report dated
December 1968 concerning the "achievements in Hue City and
surrounding districts during one year of the General Offensive and
Uprising," believed to have been prepared by the Hue City Party
Committee. Captured by the 1st RVNAF Infantry Division on
January 22, 1969.

15. Doc. Log No. 05-1131-68 (see n. 14).

16. Doc. Log No. 05-2371-68 (Confidential), summarized in
MACJ2 Bulletin No. 12,651, dated May 23, 1968. Summary of a
captured tape recording containing the achievements report of a
covert Viet Cong agent in Hue. Captured by the 1st U.S. Air Cavalry
Division on April 25, 1968. The tape also revealed the names of eight
senior GVN officials and military officers who allegedly had
"reported" to the Communists after the City was seized.

17. Doc. Log No. 05-1131-68 (see n. 14).

18. Doc. Log No. 05-2470-68 (Confidential), dated September
16, 1968. Extract translation of a "Recapitulation Report" dated
March 30, 1968, concerning the attack on Hue from January 31 to
February 25, 1968; prepared by the Commander of the 6th
Regiment, Tri-Thien-Hue Military Region. Captured by the 1st
Infantry Division, RVNAF I CTZ, on May 20, 1968.

19. *Ibid.*

20. Doc. Log No. 11-0502-68 (Confidential), dated November 26,
1968. Translation of a J2, Joint General Staff, ARVN compilation of
VC/NVA documents that were captured during 1968 in South
Vietnam.

21. Doc. Log No. 06-2049-68 (Confidential), dated October 23,
1968. Extract translation of a notebook with entries dated between
January 9 and April 12, 1968, maintained by an unidentified
military cadre who had operated in the Hue area. Captured by the 1st
U.S. Air Cavalry Division on June 12, 1968.

22. Doc. Log No. 05-1131-68 (see n. 14).

23. *Ibid.*

24. *The New York Times*, May 1, 1968, pp. 1 and 8.

25. *Ibid.*

26. *The Washington Post*, May 6, 1969, pp. A1 and A16.

27. Doc. Log No. 04-2944-68 (Confidential), summarized in MACJ2 Bulletin No. 11,791, dated April 26, 1968. Summary of an "Activity Report" dated April 10, 1968, prepared by a member of the Security Section of Quang Tri Province. This report covered security activities in Quang Tri Province from January to April 1968 and is believed to have been addressed to the Security Section of Tri-Thien-Hue Military Region. Captured by the 101st U.S. Airborne Division on April 19, 1968.

28. Doc. Log No. 06-2049-68 (see n. 21).

29. Doc. Log No. 05-1131-68 (see n. 14). There is also evidence of open Communist endorsement of what occurred in Hue. On April 27, 1969, for example, Hanoi Radio characterized the Hue victims as "hooligan lackeys who had owed blood debts to the Tri-Thien-Hue compatriots and who were annihilated by the southern armed forces and people in early Mau Than spring [Tet]."

30. Doc. Log No. 02-5276-69 (see n. 14).

31. Doc. Log No. 08-1216-66 (Confidential), summarized in MACJ2 Bulletin No. 803, dated August 11, 1966. Summary of a draft security plan prepared by an unidentified agency concerning security missions for the second half of 1965. Captured by a unit of the III MAF on July 8, 1966.

32. A captured letter dated September 10, 1968, and attributed to an agency of Military Region II headquarters called upon certain subordinate districts to recruit more personnel for their Armed Reconnaissance Units and to bring their strength up to 230 to 240 men. Doc. Log No. 02-5589-69 (Confidential), summarized in MACJ2 Bulletin No. 16, dated March 6, 1969. Captured by the 9th U.S. Infantry Division in February 1969.

33. For example, Doc. Log No. 02-1066-69 (Confidential), summarized in MACJ2 Bulletin No. 20,275, dated February 2, 1969; and Doc. Log No. 02-5612-69 (Confidential), summarized in MACJ2 Bulletin No. 15, dated March 6, 1969.

34. Doc. Log No. 07-1770-67 (see Chap. 2, n. 3).

35. Doc. Log No. 06-2310-67 (Confidential), summarized in MACJ2 Bulletin No. 5364, dated June 12, 1967. Summary of verdicts issued by the Tay Ninh Province Liberation Army between

April 28 and May 19, 1967. Captured by the 25th U.S. Infantry Division on June 6, 1967.

36. Doc. Log No. 01-2371-69 (Confidential), dated September 19, 1969. Translation of a verdict dated September 19, 1968, issued by the Phu Cat District People's Court, Binh Dinh Province. Captured by the Capital ROK Infantry Division on January 4, 1969.

37. For example, Doc. Log No. 01-2396-67 (Confidential), dated January 23, 1968. Translation of a training document on the objectives and techniques of combat reconnaissance in urban areas. Captured by the 173rd Airborne Brigade on January 14, 1967.

38. Doc. Log No. 01-1604-68 (Confidential), dated January 25, 1968. Translation of an undated training document entitled "The Task of Breaking the Enemy Control and Eliminating the Tyrants in the City." Captured by the 794th RF Company, Binh Duong Sector, RVNAF III CTZ, on January 8, 1968.

39. *Ibid.*

40. *Ibid.*

41. Doc. Log No. 07-2505-68 (Confidential), dated September 4, 1968. Translation of a notebook containing the minutes of a regimental conference on "Drawing Experience in Political and Military Tasks," believed to have been maintained by a cadre of the lst Regiment, Subregion 4. Captured by the PBR-U.S. Navy-RSSZ on July 21, 1968.

42. Doc. Log No. 09-2128-68 (Confidential), summarized in MACJ2 Bulletin No. 16,674, dated September 24, 1968. Summary of a circular dated September 4, 1968, concerning future armed and proselytizing activities in Bien Hoa Province and believed to have been issued by the Current Affairs Committee of the Bien Hoa Province Unit. Captured by the 36th Ranger Battalion, RVNAF III CTZ, on September 13, 1968.

43. Doc. Log No. 09-1365-68 (Confidential), summarized in MACJ2 Bulletin No. 16,281, dated September 6, 1968. Captured by the 82d U.S. Airborne Division on August 28, 1968.

44. Doc. Log No. 07-2213-68 (Confidential), summarized in MACJ2 Bulletin No. 14,498, dated July 18, 1968. Captured by the lst U.S. Air Cavalry Division on July 5, 1968.

45. Doc. Log No. 04-2752-68 (Confidential), summarized in MACJ2 Bulletin No. 11,701, dated April 23, 1968. Captured by the Capital ROK Infantry Division on March 23, 1968.

46. For example, Doc. Log No. 12-1767-67 (Confidential), dated March 4, 1968, and Doc. Log No. 09-2124-68 (Confidential),

summarized in MACJ2 Bulletin No. 16,670, dated September 24, 1968.

47. An example was found in Doc. Log No. 12-2411-67 (Confidential), summarized in MACJ2 Bulletin No. 8586, dated December 21, 1967. Summary of a circular dated November 5, 1967, concerning activities during the forthcoming 1967-1968 Winter and Spring campaign; prepared by the Mo Duc District Unit Headquarters, Quang Ngai Province. Captured by the 4th U.S. Infantry Division on November 27, 1967. Another directive, from the same period, is contained in Doc. Log No. 01-1728-68 (Confidential), summarized in MACJ2 Bulletin No. 8952, dated January 15, 1968. Summary of a directive dated November 10, 1967, providing guidelines for the 1967-1968 Winter -Spring campaign in Binh Dinh Province. Captured by the 1st U.S. Air Cavalry Division on November 29, 1967.

48. Doc. Log No. 01-1846-68 (Confidential), summarized in MACJ2 Bulletin No. 8997, dated January 17, 1968. Summary of a circular dated November 1, 1967, concerning preparations for taking over GVN administrative organizations in the cities, towns, and rural areas of Binh Dinh Province. This circular is believed to have been issued by the Binh Dinh Province Party Committee. Captured by the 1st U.S. Air Cavalry Division on November 30, 1967. Also, Doc. Log No. 01-1099-68 (Confidential), summarized in MACJ2 Bulletin No. 8759, dated January 3, 1967. Summary of a resolution concerning the formation of suicide cells in Quang Nam Province during November 1967. Captured by the 1st USMC Division.

49. Doc. Log No. 01-1746-68 (Confidential), summarized in MACJ2 Bulletin No. 8960, dated January 15, 1968. Summary of an undated memorandum attributed to the Phu My District Party Committee, Binh Dinh Province, concerning the activation of village suicide units in Phu My District. Captured by the 1st U.S. Air Cavalry Division on November 29, 1967.

50. Doc. Log No. 02-1290-68 (see Chap. 2, n. 64).

51. For example, Doc. Log No. 08-2105-68 (Confidential), summarized in MACJ2 Bulletin No. 15,622, dated August 18, 1968, and Doc. Log No. 09-2147-68 (Confidential), summarized in MACJ2 Bulletin No. 16,681, dated September 24, 1968.

52. Doc. Log No. 08-2472-68 (Confidential), in MACJ2 Bulletin No. 15,822, dated August 25, 1968. Translation of a directive dated August 8, 1968, concerning preparations for the Third General Offensive in Quang Ngai Province. This directive is attributed to the

149

Duc Pho District Unit Headquarters, Quang Ngai Province. Captured by the Americal Division on August 11, 1968.

53. Doc. Log No. 10-1679-66 (see Chap. 2, n. 3).

54. Doc. Log No. 07-1770-67 (see Chap. 2, n. 3).

55. *Ibid.*

56. *Ibid.*

57. *Ibid.*

58. Doc. Log No. 10-1679-66 and Doc. Log No. 07-1770-67 (see Chap. 2, n. 3).

59. Doc. Log No. 12-1768-66 (Confidential), dated January 27, 1967. Translation of a quarterly report dated September 19, 1966, prepared by an unidentified village security agency. Captured by the 5th SFGA on December 3, 1966.

60. Doc. Log No. 07-1092-66 (see Chap. 2, n. 56) and Doc. Log No. 07-1770-67 (see Chap. 2, n. 3).

61. Doc. Log No. 07-1770-67 (see Chap. 2, n. 3).

62. Doc. Log No. 07-1092-66 (see Chap. 2, n. 56).

63. Doc. Log No. 10-1679-66 (see Chap. 2, n. 3).

64. RM-5267/2-ISA/ARPA, *Some Observations on Viet Cong Operations in the Villages*, by W.P. Davison, May 1968, p. 37. In this revealing study of Communist village-level operations, Davison (pp. 34-35) describes the treatment afforded one former government official during several "reduction-in-prestige" sessions:

After his village was overrun, he was taken to the mountains and subjected to intensive indoctrination. Then he was ordered to write out a declaration telling about all his activities since 1954, all the positions he had occupied in the government administration, how many underground cadres he had helped to arrest, and how many secret Viet Cong organizations he had helped the government authorities to uncover. He also had to describe the activities of his parents, brothers, and sisters.

After he had completed this document, he was taken back to the village and a "condemnation meeting" was assembled. There he had to read his declaration before the villagers, and the cadres asked the people whether he had told the full truth, and whether he had actually committed any other "crimes." Those present were urged to denounce him if he had not told the truth.

In this case, the villagers remained silent, so the cadres assembled a second meeting at which the accused was not present. Apparently urged on by Viet Cong authorities, several villagers denounced the former official for vague crimes, such as general abuse of power or arrogance. These accusations were then read at still a third gathering—this one a general meeting of the entire population. As the source described it, "the cadres wanted to debase us in the eyes of the villagers."

65. Doc. Log No. 07-1770-67 (see Chap. 2, n. 3).

66. Doc. Log No. 09-1357-67 (Confidential), dated November 7, 1967. Translation of a roster of 685 individuals arrested by the Viet Cong in seven villages of Duc Pho District, Quang Ngai Province, during 1965, 1966, and the first three months of 1967. Among other information, the roster includes the name, age, residence, religion, education, social class, date and place of arrest, and the "crime" committed by each individual. Captured by the 1st U.S. Infantry Division on August 16, 1967.

67. Doc. Log No. 10-1679-66 (see Chap. 2, n. 3).

68. Doc. Log No. 09-1275-67 (Confidential), dated December 30, 1967. Translation of a letter dated March 27, 1967, concerning the transfer of seventeen prisoners to a thought-reform camp in an unidentified province. Captured by the 1st U.S. Infantry Division on August 16, 1967.

69. Doc. Log No. 08-3652-67 (Confidential), dated January 9, 1968. Translation of a "Directive on the Execution of the Policy Toward Prisoners and Surrenderers" produced by the Political Staff, Work Site 5, SVN Liberation Army. Captured by the 9th U.S. Infantry Division on August 22, 1967. A report on a prisoner who was killed in February 1968 for refusing to make a declaration during his interrogation was found in Doc. Log No. 04-3213-68 (Confidential), summarized in MACJ2 Bulletin No. 11,932, dated April 30, 1968.

70. Doc. Log No. 10-1679-66 (see Chap. 2, n. 3). For a report on the torture of prisoners in a Viet Cong prison, see Doc. Log No. 05-1582-66 (Confidential), summarized in MACJ2 Bulletin No. 465, dated May 29, 1966. The summary is of an "Inspection Report" on the prison camp in Duc Phong District, Phuoc Long Province. Captured by the 101st U.S. Airborne Division on May 17, 1966.

71. The severity of the punishment meted out to an individual depends first and foremost on the nature and seriousness of his "crimes." But sentences are also influenced by the individual's ideological attitude and social class; his willingness to "repent," confess all "crimes," and undergo "reform"; and his "political influence" (that is, his standing within the community). E.g., Doc. Log Nos. 07-1770-67 and 10-1679-66 (see Chap. 2, n. 3).

72. Doc. Log No. 10-1679-66 (see Chap. 2, n. 3).

73. Doc. Log No. 07-1092-66 (see Chap. 2, n. 56).

74. Doc. Log No. 04-2944-68 (see n. 27). Another, more recent example of executions authorized at the village level is contained in Doc. Log No. 06-1939-69 (see Chap. 2, n. 7).

75. According to the captured minutes of a meeting held by cadres of Military Region V from March 1 to 4, 1966, a total of 5,753 RVNAF servicemen were captured as prisoners of war in MR V during 1965. Of these, 4,601 were released, 16 were turned over to Security Sections, 18 died of sickness, and 181 volunteered to join Viet Cong units. At the time of the meeting, some 846 POWs were being detained in various provincial detention camps. Doc. Log No. 04-1707-67 (Confidential), summarized in MACJ2 Bulletin No. 3635, dated April 9, 1967. Captured by the U.S. 1st Air Cavalry Division on March 29, 1967.

76. Doc. Log No. 12-2312-68 (Confidential), dated January 28, 1969. Translation of a draft statement dated October 19, 1966, on standard operating procedures (including the handling of prisoners of war) in Quang Ngai Province. Captured by the Americal Division on January 1, 1969.

77. Doc. Log No. 05-1157-68 (Confidential), summarized in MACJ2 Bulletin No. 12,028, dated May 3, 1968. Summary of a report dated June 15, 1967, from a district detention camp in Quang Nam Province. Captured by the Americal Division on March 12, 1968.

78. Doc. Log No. 06-1329-66 (Confidential), summarized in MACJ2 Bulletin No. 573, dated June 24, 1966. Summary of an activity report for the first quarter of 1966, dated March 27, 1966, and prepared by the Security Section of Soc Trang Province. Captured by the RVNAF 21st Infantry Division on May 14, 1966.

79. Doc. Log No. 08-1897-67 (Confidential), dated December 7, 1967. Translation of roster of 123 persons (including the "crimes" of each individual) who had been imprisoned in a district detention camp in Phu Yen Province between 1965 and early 1967. Captured by the 9th ROK Infantry Division on August 3, 1967.

80. Doc. Log No. 10-1679-66 (see Chap. 2, n. 3).

81. *Ibid.*

82. For example, five rosters, dated between December 17, 1966, and May 5, 1967, from a thought-reform camp in Binh Dinh Province revealed that 70 of the 100 civilian suspects who had been arrested and detained at the camp between July 28, 1966, and March 30, 1967, were released after a period of indoctrination. Doc. Log No. 09-1330-67 (Confidential), summarized in MACJ2 Bulletin No. 7174, dated September 9, 1967. Captured by the 1st U.S. Air Cavalry Division on August 16, 1967.

83. Doc. Log No. 08-1954-67 (Confidential), dated December 14,

1967. Translation of several rosters, dated September 1966, of persons who were detained at, escaped from, or were executed at the Tuy Hoa I District Thought-Reform Camp in Phu Yen Province. The rosters contain biographical data on each individual (including his "crimes" and political affiliations, if any) and the sentences meted out to each. Captured by the 9th ROK Infantry Division on August 3, 1967.

84. *Ibid.* Another example is Doc. Log No. 08-1894-67 (Confidential), dated December 31, 1967. Translation of a roster dated May 1, 1966, listing 99 persons detained at the Tuy Hoa I District Thought-Reform Camp from September 5, 1964, to January 22, 1966. This roster also presents the "crimes" and length of sentence for each individual, and includes a biographical sketch outlining his or her past activities and progress while undergoing reform. Captured by the 9th ROK Infantry Division on August 3, 1967.

85. *Ibid.*

86. Prisoner populations are derived from the following provincial reports: Ca Mau Province, Doc. Log No. 06-1338-66 (see Chap. 3, n. 43); Rach Gia Province, Doc. Log No. 06-1282-66 (Confidential), summarized in MACJ2 Bulletin No. 558, dated June 22, 1966 (summary of a security status report for 1965 dated January 23, 1966, issued by the Commander of the Rach Gia Security Section, and captured by the 21st RVNAF Infantry Division on May 14, 1966); Ba Xuyen, Doc. Log No. 06-1169-66 (Confidential), summarized in MACJ2 Bulletin No. 521, dated June 14, 1966 (summary of a security report for the first quarter of 1966 prepared by the Security Section of Ba Xuyen Province, and captured by the 21st RVNAF Infantry Division on May 14, 1966); Soc Trang, Doc. Log No. 06-1329-66 (see n. 78); and Ca Mau (1968), Doc. Log No. 12-1476-68 (Confidential), summarized in MACJ2 Bulletin No. 18,569, dated December 10, 1968. (The last is a summary of a draft plan dated June 13, 1968, which discloses the number of persons detained at various provincial and district thought-reform camps in Ca Mau Province, and indicates that most of them had been arrested for antirevolutionary attitudes. Captured by the IV CTZ 6799 on December 8, 1968.)

87. Doc. Log No. 08-1421-68 (Confidential), summarized in MACJ2 Bulletin No. 15,257, dated August 7, 1968. Summary of a report dated April 24, 1967, and attributed to an element of the Quang Tri Province Security Section. Captured by the 1st U.S. Air Cavalry Division on July 25, 1968.

88. The captured notebook of a security cadre in Hoai Nhon District, Binh Duong Province, for example, indicates that, by the end of October 1964, 207 prisoners had been freed from the District's thought- reform camp and only 102 prisoners remained in the camp. Doc. Log No. 05-1608-66 (Confidential), summarized in MACJ2 Bulletin No. 471, dated June 2, 1966. Captured by the U.S. 1st Air Cavalry Division on May 4, 1966.

89. A report dated May 19, 1968, and attributed to the Security Section of Subregion 1, for example, stated that most of the prisoners held in the Subregion's detention camps suffered from cholera or beriberi. Doc. Log No. 01-1097-69 (Confidential), summarized in MACJ2 Bulletin No. 19,213, dated January 2, 1969. Captured by the 25th U.S. Infantry Division on December 13, 1968.

90. Doc. Log No. 08-1421-68 (see n. 87).

91. According to a captured letter dated April 26, 1966, from the COSVN Security Section, three important prisoners held at one Communist base area were to be killed if an impending Allied sweep operation were to force the evacuation of the base. Doc. Log No. 03-2668-67 (Confidential), summarized in MACJ2 Bulletin No. 3149, dated March 23, 1967. Captured by the 25th U.S. Infantry Division. A report of a prisoner who was actually killed during an Allied sweep operation against a detention camp is contained in Doc. Log No. 01-1853-68 (Confidential), summarized in MACJ2 Bulletin No. 8999, dated January 17, 1968.

92. Doc. Log No. 09-1197-67 (Confidential), summarized in MACJ2 Bulletin No. 7143, dated September 7, 1967. Summary of a document dated April 27, 1967, prepared by the Security Section of Quang Ngai Province and describing the mission and responsibilities of the Armed Security Service in the administration of detention camps. Captured by the 101st U.S. Airborne Division on September 1, 1967. Also, Doc. Log No. 12-1475-68 (Confidential), summarized in MACJ2 Bulletin No. 18,568, dated December 10, 1968. Summary of a document outling the regulations to be observed by inmates of a detention camp believed to have been in Cai Nuoc District, Ca Mau Province. Captured by the IV CTZ 6799 on December 8, 1968.

93. Information on the penalties suffered by "uncooperative" prisoners is derived from an interrogation report of an ARVN officer who had been in several Viet Cong detention camps prior to his escape in September 1968. CMIC Report No. 6028-5640-68 (Confidential), dated November 26, 1968.

94. Doc. Log No. 08-1894-67 (see n. 84).

95. Doc. Log No. 10-1679-66 (see Chap. 2, n. 3).

96. Doc. Log No. 08-1249-66 (Confidential), summarized in MACJ2 Bulletin No. 808, dated August 12, 1966. Summary of the dossiers of 147 persons who were arrested and sentenced in Binh Khe District, Binh Dinh Province, during 1965. Captured by the 1st U.S. Air Cavalry Division on June 1, 1966.

97. Doc. Log No. 08-1666-67 (Confidential), dated January 12, 1968. Translation of rosters of 158 persons detained and punished in the Tuy Hoa II District Thought-Reform Camp, Phu Yen Province. The rosters contained detailed biographic data (social class, education, religion, political party affiliation, etc.) along with the "crimes" committed, and specified the sentence handed down to each person. Captured by the 4th U.S. Infantry Division.

98. Examples of the types of persons executed are provided by the following: Doc. Log No. 05-1608-66 (see n. 88); Doc. Log No. 08-1954-67 (see n. 83); Doc. Log No. 11-1867-68 (Confidential), summarized in MACJ2 Bulletin No. 18,086, dated November 22, 1968; Doc. Log No. 12-1798-67 (Confidential), summarized in MACJ2 Bulletin No. 8431, dated December 13, 1967; Doc. Log No. 12-2267-68 (Confidential), summarized in MACJ2 Bulletin No. 19,061, dated December 28, 1968; and Doc. Log No. 01-2378-69 (Confidential), summarized in MACJ2 Bulletin No. 19,962, dated January 24, 1969.

99. Doc. Log No. 08-1954-67 (see n. 83).

100. Doc. Log No. 06-1282-66 (see n. 86).

101. Doc. Log No. 06-1338-66 (see Chap. 3, n. 43).

102. Doc. Log No. 08-1249-66 (see n. 96).

103. Doc. Log No. 04-2004-68 (Confidential), summarized in MACJ2 Bulletin No. 11,323, dated April 12, 1968. Summary of a notebook with entries dated between December 25, 1966, and June 21, 1967, maintained by a member of the Security Section, Binh Tan District, Saigon-Gia Dinh Military Region. Captured by the 9th U.S. Infantry Division on March 2, 1968.

104. Doc. Log No. 12-1370-68 (Confidential). Translation of a "Special Directive" dated November 20, 1968, issued by the Security Section, People's Revolutionary Council, Trang Bang District, Subregion 1. Captured by the 25th U.S. Infantry Division on December 3, 1968.

105. Doc. Log No. 10-1679-66 (see Chap. 2, n. 3).

106. Doc. Log No. 08-1421-68 (see n. 87).

107. Execution by stabbing was reported in the case of a GVN

informant, accused of supplying information to the Gia Dinh Province Chieu Hoi Center, who was arrested in December 1967. (Doc. Log No. 03-1191-68 [Confidential], summarized in MACJ2 Bulletin No. 10,026, dated March 4, 1968. Summary of a report dated December 12, 1967, on the interrogation of GVN informant Nguyen Van Su, prepared by a cadre of the Security Section, Subregion 1, and captured by the 25th U.S. Infantry Division on March 1, 1968.) In another instance, a victim reportedly was beaten to death by the Viet Cong; in a letter dated August 23, 1968, and addressed to the Anh Tinh Village Party Chapter, Trang Bang District, Subregion 1, a woman living in An Thoi Hamlet, Anh Tinh Village, said that on April 12, 1968, her husband had been apprehended by Viet Cong cadres and beaten to death at a location 1,500 meters from their home. She expressed bitterness about this inhuman act, which she described as murder caused by personal rancor. (Doc. Log No. 01-2729-69 [Confidential], summarized in MACJ2 Bulletin No. 20,177, dated January 30, 1969; captured by the 25th U.S. Infantry Division on January 26, 1969.)

108. Doc. Log No. 06-1338-66 (see Chap. 3, n. 43).

109. Doc. Log No. 06-1282-66 (see n. 86).

110. Doc. Log No. 06-2386-67 (Confidential), dated July 29, 1967. Translation of seven letters, dated between February and May 1967, concerning security operations in various village and district Security Sections of Thua Thien Province. Captured by units of the III MAF on June 7, 1967.

111. Doc. Log No. 01-2624-67 (see Chap. 3, n. 5).

112. *Ibid.*

113. Doc. Log No. 01-2820-69 (Confidential), summarized in MACJ2 Bulletin No. 20,232, dated January 31, 1969. Summary of a Secret report dated December 13, 1968 (concerning various security activities in Subregion 1 during October and November 1968), attributed to an unidentified agency of Subregion 1. Captured by the 25th U.S. Infantry Division on January 26, 1969.

114. Doc. Log No. 02-1176-69 (Confidential), dated April 5, 1969. Translation of a Secret report dated January 6, 1969 ("on the enemy situation and the security tasks in Military Region I during December 1968"), attributed to the Security Section of Subregion 1. Captured by the 25th U.S. Infantry Division on January 26, 1969.

115. Doc. Log No. 01-3347-67 (see Chap. 2, n. 49).

116. Doc. Log No. 03-2434-68 (Confidential), in MACJ2 Bulletin No. 10,647, dated March 23, 1968. Translation of a letter dated

February 1968 from COSVN to Saigon-Cholon-Gia Dinh Region Headquarters containing an evaluation of the first days of the General Offensive. Captured by the 1st U.S. Infantry Division on March 13, 1968.

117. Doc. Log No. 03-2497-68 (see n. 9).

118. Doc. Log No. 12-1196-68 (Confidential), dated January 14, 1969. Translation of an "After-action Report on Combat Activities" in May 1968, attributed to an element of the Dong Nai Regiment, Headquarters, Subregion 5. Captured by the 11th U.S. ACR on December 2, 1968.

119. Doc. Log No. 04-2435-68 (see Chap. 2, n. 26).

120. Doc. Log No. 07-2373-68 (Confidential), summarized in MACJ2 Bulletin No. 14,575, dated July 20, 1968. Summary of a circular dated May 16, 1968, concerning the need to step up the annihilation of GVN officials, intelligence agents, and informants living in cities and hamlets in "liberated," contested, and GVN-controlled areas. Attributed to the Security Section of Subregion 5, the circular was addressed to subordinate district sections. Captured by the Binh Duong Sector, RVNAF III CTZ, on June 10, 1968.

121. For example, Doc. Log No. 12-1696-68 (Confidential), summarized in MACJ2 Bulletin No. 18,716, dated December 14, 1968. Summary of a circular dated November 19, 1968, concerning the total failure of many areas to break the enemy's oppressive control and to annihilate tyrants and local administration personnel. Attributed to the Dien Ban District Party Committee, Quang Da Special Zone. Captured by the 1st USMC Division on November 27, 1968.

122. Doc. Log No. 12-1954-68 (Confidential), summarized in MACJ2 Bulletin No. 18,876, dated December 19, 1968. Summary of a Top Secret directive, dated December 3, 1968 (attributed to the Current Affairs Committee, Quang Nam Province), which criticizes the failure of subordinate units to destroy the government's refugee resettlement centers and annihilate its administrative, pacification, and intelligence personnel so as to liberate the rural areas. Captured by ROK Marine Forces on December 4, 1968.

123. Doc. Log No. 04-2944-68 (see n. 27).

124. Doc. Log No. 03-2497-68 (see n. 9).

125. *Ibid.*

126. *The New York Times*, January 19, 1969, p. 4.

127. Doc. Log No. 10-2187-68 (see Chap. 2, n. 13).

128. Doc. Log No. 03-2042-68 (Confidential), dated March 30,

1968. Translation of a Secret training document entitled "Experiences in the Build-up of Armed Forces in Cities," published in 1967 by the Binh Tan Propaganda and Training Section, Subregion 2. Captured by the 25th U.S. Infantry Division on March 14, 1968.

129. Doc. Log No. 11-2036-68 (Confidential), dated December 23, 1968. Translation of a report dated June 1968, "On the Results of the Inspection of the Security Measures in Go Dau [District]," prepared by the chief of the Administrative Section, Tay Ninh Province Security Section. Captured by the 25th U.S. Infantry Division on November 23, 1968.

130. Doc. Log No. 10-1599-68 (Confidential), dated November 2, 1968. Translation of a report dated August 30, 1968, addressed to the Current Affairs Committee of T3, believed to have been prepared by a covert cadre operating in the 7th Precinct of Saigon. Captured by the 199th U.S. Light Infantry Brigade.

131. Doc. Log No. 08-2872-68 (Confidential), summarized in MACJ2 Bulletin No. 16,061, dated August 31, 1968. Summary of a notebook containing entries dated between April 17, 1967, and May 18, 1968, and maintained by a cadre of the Ba To District Unit, Quang Ngai Province. Captured by the 5th U.S. SFGA on August 8, 1968.

Chapter 5
The Alternative to Repression

1. Doc. Log No. 07-1770-67 (see Chap. 2, n. 3).
2. *Ibid.*, and Doc. Log No. 01-3347-67 (see Chap. 2, n. 49).
3. A directive produced on August 8, 1967, by an unidentified agency outlined some regulations governing the control and handling of secret agents (fifth-columnists) recruited from GVN ranks. Chiefs and assistant chiefs of provincial and regional Security Sections were to control all secret agents recruited from those now serving the "puppet" regime, such as policemen, company-grade officers, district officials, and clerks. But only the chief and the assistant chief of the Military Region Security Section were to be responsible for the more senior agents, such as field-grade officers, intellectuals, and high-ranking officials. The directive went on to state that those secret agents who scored achievements should be encouraged to join the Party; those who sacrificed their lives in the service of the Revolution were to be honored, and their families provided with material assistance

by the Viet Cong. Doc. Log No. 12-2958-67 (Confidential), summarized in MACJ2 Bulletin No. 8721, dated December 30, 1967. Captured by the 974th RF Company, RVNAF IV CTZ, on September 25, 1967. Party membership, however, is by no means open to all former GVN persons. According to another directive, issued by the Political Department, Central Rear Service Department, NVA, on August 28, 1967, it is never to be granted to: former members of the VNQDD and Dai Viet parties; former RVNAF informers or officers and enlisted men who have committed oppressive acts against the population; and individuals whose close relatives have committed crimes against the populace. Doc. Log No. 05-2657-68 (Confidential), summarized in MACJ2 Bulletin No. 12,798, dated May 28, 1968. Captured by the 1st U.S. Air Cavalry Division on May 7, 1968.

4. For example, Doc. Log No. 07-2928-68 (see Chap. 3, n. 16).

5. Examples of Communist concern about false GVN defectors attempting to infiltrate their ranks were found in Doc. Log No. 07-2253-68 (Confidential), summarized in MACJ2 Bulletin No. 14,517, dated July 19, 1968, and Doc. Log No. 09-1531-68 (Confidential), summarized in MACJ2 Bulletin No. 16,362, dated September 10, 1968. In order to tighten security and "to frustrate the enemy plot of employing penetration agents to undermine our organization," the SVN People's Liberation Army Headquarters issued a directive on April 5, 1968, concerning the regulations to be followed on the "recruitment of personnel into the Liberation Army." It stipulated that "the biographical data of the recruits of the Liberation Army must be clear-cut" and that all recruits must be "confident in the leadership of the Lao Dong Party and faithful to the Revolution and the Fatherland." More specifically, "none of the following individuals will be recruited":

1) Individuals who physically and intentionally served the "U.S." imperialists and their henchmen as spies and informants, thereby causing heavy losses to the Revolution and the people.

2) Members of Anti-Communist Political Parties, such as the Labor and Personal Dignity [Can Lao Nhan Vi] Party, Nationalist [Dai Viet] Party, and Vietnamese Nationalist [Viet Nam Quoc Dan Dang] Party, leaders of other enemy organizations, and cruel tyrants whose thoughts and acts are against the Revolution.

3) Individuals who have really participated in the U.S. and puppet political, military, economic, cultural, and social organizations, or cruel tyrants whose activities are prejudicial to the Revolution.

4) Individuals who surrendered to the enemy, betrayed their fatherland, or those who, after being captured by the enemy, made noxious statements to the detriment of the Revolution and people.

5) Delinquent individuals who are not yet at the level of political awareness, such as hooligans, vagabonds, and prostitutes.

6) Those who nurse a grudge or oppose the Revolution due to the execution of their next of kin or relatives by the Party.

7) Individuals whose relatives are wicked tyrants, Canton chiefs, District chiefs, Province chiefs, Province deputy chiefs, personnel subordinate to espionage and intelligence services, policemen, public security agents, spies, or special force soldiers. Also excluded are puppet officers, mercantile bourgeois, and other reactionary elements who still maintain a close association with the above individuals, and/or have reactionary political views, those who are easily bought by the enemy, and/or those who may betray their fatherland.

8) Individuals who do not fall within one of the above categories, but whose past activities and private lives are not clear-cut; their recruitment is not approved by the majority.

Doc. Log No. 02-1717-69 (Confidential), dated February 28, 1969. Captured by the CTU 194.9.5, U.S. Navy, on February 16, 1969.

6. "Political Program of the South Vietnam National Front for Liberation," Hanoi Radio (VNA International News Service), September 1, 1967.

7. For example, Doc. Log No. 04-2173-68 (Confidential), summarized in MACJ2 Bulletin No. 11,401, dated April 15, 1968; Doc. Log No. 03-2746-68 (Confidential), summarized in MACJ2 Bulletin No. 10,786, dated March 28, 1968; and Doc. Log No. 01-1135-68 (Confidential), summarized in MACJ2 Bulletin No. 8771, dated January 4, 1968.

8. Doc. Log No. 07-2418-68 (Confidential), dated August 13, 1968. Extract translation of a directive containing the "Nine-Point Policies Regarding the Newly Liberated Cities," issued by the Political Staff, B 3 Front, on February 10, 1968. Captured by the 11th U.S. ACR between July 18 and 19, 1968. Other captured documents relating to these "Nine-Point Policies" are Doc. Log No. 02-2020-68 (Confidential), summarized in MACJ2 Bulletin No. 9757, dated February 25, 1968; Doc. Log No. 03-1207-68 (Confidential), summarized in MACJ2 Bulletin No. 10,034, dated March 4, 1968; and Doc. Log No. 02-1986-68 (Confidential), summarized in MACJ2 Bulletin No. 9740, dated February 24, 1968.

9. Doc. Log No. 02-1823-68 (Confidential), dated February 27, 1968. Translation of a 1968 "Order" issued by the Revolutionary Council of the Anti-Thieu/Ky Civilian and Military United Forces of Khanh Hoa Province. Captured by the 50th MP, I FFV, on January 30, 1968.

10. "Statement by the Provisional Revolutionary Government of the Republic of South Vietnam on Its Program of Action," *Hoc Tap*, No. 6, June 1969, as translated in JPRS, *Translations on North Vietnam*, No. 583, pp. 26-32.

11. Doc. Log No. 02-2080-68 (Confidential), dated March 4, 1968. Translation of a directive on political and proselytizing activities, issued by an unidentified Communist agency on February 9, 1968. Captured by the 9th U.S. Infantry Division.

12. Doc. Log No. 04-2018-68 (Confidential), dated April 29, 1968. Translation containing the text of a surrender leaflet issued in the name of the "Partisan Group of Thanh Noi [Hue Citadel] District." Captured by the 82d U.S. Airborne Division on March 20, 1968.

13. One example of this is provided in a directive concerning the use of "teenage" spies by the GVN, issued to the district Security Sections of Subregion 4 on November 25, 1968, by the Security Section of Subregion 4. Warning that the enemy was recruiting "children between 10 and 15 years of age into his intelligence agencies," the directive ordered district echelons to put a stop to this practice by requiring parents to indoctrinate their children "not to work for the enemy." It went on: "The parents will stand as guardians of the youth. If the parents of the young man are a bad element, the Village Security should seriously warn them and require them to guarantee that their child will stop serving the enemy. If they do not do as promised and their child continues serving the enemy, they will be punished according to the seriousness of their fault." Doc. Log No. 02-1119-69 (Confidential), dated February 20, 1969. Captured by D/1/RAR, 1st ATF, on January 14, 1969. Viet Cong agitation and propaganda cadres are instructed to tell the parents of GVN military personnel that they themselves become "Vietnamese traitors if their children serve in the enemy army." Doc. Log No. 09-2353-68 (Confidential), dated October 4, 1968. Translation of an activity report dated August 18, 1968, attributed to the Nha Be District Unit, Subregion 3. Captured by the 9th U.S. Infantry Division on September 18, 1968.

14. Doc. Log No. 07-1770-67 (see Chap. 2, n. 3).

15. Doc. Log No. 01-1057-69 (Confidential), dated January 31, 1969. Translation of a "Resolution" dated December 4, 1968, concerning various activities planned for December 1968 in Nam Can District, believed to have been prepared by the Nam Can District Party Committee, Ca Mau Province. Captured by Silver Mace, U.S. Navy, on December 21, 1968. Another statement on the sending of "warning notices enumerating the crimes committed by the tyrants" was found in Doc. Log No. 09-2353-68 (see n. 13).

16. Doc. Log No. 07-3166-68 (Confidential), summarized in MACJ2 Bulletin No. 14,973, dated July 30, 1968. Summary of a "Public Denunciation" dated May 14, 1968, issued by the National Liberation Front Committee of Tan An District. Captured by the 173d U.S. Airborne Brigade on May 18, 1968.

17. Doc. Log No. 05-2754-68 (Confidential), dated June 8, 1968. Translation of a Secret directive entitled "On the Strong Repression of Nationalist Party Members," issued by Agency T.775 (Quang Ngai Province) on March 29, 1968. Captured by the Americal Division in April 1968.

18. Doc. Log No. 07-2646-68 (Confidential), summarized in MACJ2 Bulletin No. 14,729, dated July 24, 1968; Doc. Log No. 04-2422-68 (Confidential), summarized in MACJ2 Bulletin No. 11,532, dated April 18, 1968; and Doc. Log No. 08-2058-68 (Confidential), dated October 18, 1968.

19. Doc. Log No. 10-2182-68 (Confidential), dated October 30, 1968. Translation of a directive dated October 9, 1968, concerning security activities to be carried out during a forthcoming General Offensive in towns and cities; believed to have been addressed to district agencies in Gia Lai Province, B 3 Front. Captured by the 477th RF Company, RVNAF II CTZ, on October 18, 1968.

20. *Ibid.*, emphasis added.

21. *Ibid.*, emphasis added.

22. Doc. Log No. 02-1148-68 (Confidential), summarized in MACJ2 Bulletin No. 9330, dated February 6, 1968. Summary of a Top Secret directive concerning proselytizing activities during the Offensive and Uprising against cities and towns, issued by the Political Department, Headquarters, Military Region V, on November 10, 1967. Captured by elements of the RVNAF II CTZ between February 1 and 3, 1968.

23. Doc. Log No. 05-2754-68 (see n. 17).

24. Doc. Log No. 11-1747-67 (Confidential), summarized in MACJ2 Bulletin No. 8013, dated November 15, 1967. Summary of a

directive concerning the disruption of the newly elected GVN village and hamlet administrations, issued to Communist village agencies in Chau Duc District on May 12, 1967. Captured by the B/7/RAR, 1st ATF, on November 1, 1967.

25. For example, Doc. Log No. 07-1067-68 (Confidential), summarized in MACJ2 Bulletin No. 13,891, dated July 2, 1968. Summary of a notebook with entries dated between December 6, 1967, and March 30, 1968, believed to have been maintained by a cadre of the Thua Thien Province Security Section. Captured by the 101st U.S. Airborne Division on June 8, 1968.

26. Doc. Log No. 01-1847-70 (Confidential), summarized in MACJ2 Bulletin No. 28,424, dated January 17, 1970. Summary of a letter dated December 12, 1969, addressed to the chief of a hamlet believed to be in Phu Cat District, Binh Dinh Province. Captured by the Capital ROK Infantry Division on December 27, 1969.

27. Doc. Log No. 04-2435-68, emphasis added (see Chap. 2, n. 26).

28. Doc. Log No. 06-1939-69 (see Chap. 2, n. 7).

29. Doc. Log No. 04-1354-68 (Confidential), summarized in MACJ2 Bulletin No. 11,030, dated April 5, 1968. Summary of a letter dated March 3, 1968, signed by a cadre of the My Thanh Dong Village Front, Duc Hue District, Hau Nghia Province. Captured by the 5th U.S. SFGA on March 28, 1968.

30. Doc. Log No. 06-2153-68 (Confidential), summarized in MACJ2 Bulletin No. 13,530, dated June 21, 1968. Summary of a Secret report dated February 23, 1968, concerning various Security Service activities, attributed to the Political Staff, Quang Da Special Zone, Military Region V. Captured by the 1st USMC Division on June 11, 1968.

31. Doc. Log No. 04-1073-68 (Confidential), summarized in MACJ2 Bulletin No. 10,904, dated April 1, 1968. Summary of a Top Secret report dated December 26, 1967, which recapitulates Communist activities between November 25 and December 26, 1967, in Cu Chi, Ben Cat, and Dau Tieng Districts, Subregion 1. Captured by the 1st U.S. Infantry Division on March 25, 1968.

32. Doc. Log No. 10-1006-68 (Confidential), summarized in MACJ2 Bulletin No. 16,809, dated October 1, 1968, and Doc. Log No. 07-2748-68 (Confidential), summarized in MACJ2 Bulletin No. 14,783, dated July 25, 1968. Examples of other documents containing similar claims were found in Doc. Log No. 03-2933-68 (Confidential), summarized in MACJ2 Bulletin No. 10,866, dated March 31, 1968; Doc. Log No. 11-1641-68 (Confidential), summarized in MACJ2 Bulletin No. 17,962, dated November 15, 1968; and Doc. Log No. 02-1244-68 (Confidential), dated February 9, 1968.

33. Doc. Log No. 05-2371-68 (see Chap. 4, n. 16).

34. Doc. Log No. 04-2955-68 (Confidential), summarized in MACJ2 Bulletin No. 11,795, dated April 26, 1968. Summary of a letter relating to the arrest of four GVN officials in My Phong Village, signed by the Ba Ra Security Section on August 9, 1967. Captured by the 9th U.S. Infantry Division on April 14, 1968.

35. Doc. Log No. 04-3044-68 (Confidential), summarized in MACJ2 Bulletin No. 11,842, dated April 28, 1968. Summary of a letter dated 1967 by the Phuoc Khanh Village Front Committee (Nhon Trach District, Subregion 4), addressed to a GVN policeman in the Phuoc Khanh police station. Captured by the 908th RF Company, III CTZ, on April 20, 1968.

36. An example is Article III of the September 19, 1968, declaration issued by the "People's Court of Phu Cat District [Binh Dinh Province]." Doc. Log No. 01-2371-69 (see Chap. 4, n. 36).

37. Doc. Log No. 03-1443-68 (Confidential), dated March 23, 1968. Translation of a draft document concerning Viet Cong policies and missions in Go Mon District, Subregion 1, from October 1967 to June 1968. Captured by the 25th U.S. Infantry Division on March 1, 1968.

38. Doc. Log No. 12-2742-67 (Confidential), dated January 9, 1968. Translation of "The Troop and Enemy Proselyting Plan for 1967," issued by an agency of Binh Dinh Province on March 4, 1967. Captured by the Combined Intelligence Company, Binh Dinh Sector, RVNAF II CTZ, on November 9, 1967.

Chapter 6
Some Implications for the Future

1. For the most comprehensive account of the Land Reform campaign, see Hoang Van Chi, *From Colonialism to Communism—A Case History of North Vietnam*, Frederick A. Praeger, New York, 1964. Another first-hand description is provided in Gérard Tongas, *J'ai Vécu dans l'Enfer Communiste au Nord Viet-Nam*, Nouvelles Editions Debresse, Paris, 1960.

2. Hoang Van Chi, *From Colonialism to Communism*, pp. 102, 171-177, and 180-191.

3. *Ibid.*, p. 196.

4. *Ibid.*, p. 185.

5. *Ibid.*, p. 212.

6. *Ibid.*, p. 163.

7. Gérard Tongas is quite explicit on the matter of reprisals, stating that the Land Reform served as an excuse for retaliation against those who had worked with the French. He charges that the targets of the Reform were frequently those who had held some kind of position, no matter how insignificant, under the French regime, and reports that he personally knew of many such cases. As one example he cites the execution of a 73-year-old village chief, who owned no land other than a tiny vegetable patch surrounding his home. *J'ai Vécu dans l'Enfer Communiste*, p. 222.

8. Hoang Van Chi, *From Colonialism to Communism*, p. 173.

9. Joseph Buttinger, *Vietnam: A Dragon Embattled*, Vol. 2: *Vietnam at War,* Frederick A. Praeger, New York, 1967, p. 914.

10. Bernard B. Fall, *The Two Viet-Nams* (2nd rev. ed.), Frederick A. Praeger, New York, 1967, pp. 155-156.

11. P.J. Honey, *Communism in North Vietnam*, The M.I.T. Press, Cambridge, Mass., 1963, p. 33.

12. Tongas, *J'ai Vécu dans l'Enfer Communiste*, p. 222.

13. Hoang Van Chi, *From Colonialism to Communism*, p. 72.

14. *Ibid.*, p. 166.

15. *Ibid.*, pp. 166-167.

16. One statement on the confiscation of "land owned by traitors or wicked tyrants" is contained in Doc. Log No. 01-2188-69 (Confidential), dated January 31, 1969. Translation of a memorandum dated October 13, 1968, concerning the activities to be carried out by village cadres upon the establishment of village administrative organizations in My Tho Province. Captured by the 9th U.S. Infantry Division. A leaflet dated February 10, 1968, issued in the name of "United Front for Peace and Nationalism" in Quang Ngai Province, warned that all property of intransigent officials would be confiscated when the Saigon administration was overthrown. Doc. Log No. 07-2206-68 (Unclassified), summarized in MACJ2 Bulletin No. 14,494, dated July 18, 1968. Captured by the Americal Division on April 27, 1968.

17. *The Washington Evening Star*, July 13, 1969, p. A2.

18. Stewart Alsop, "Is the War Lost?" *Newsweek*, May 5, 1969, p. 120.

19. Doc. Log No. 07-1770-67, original emphasis (see Chap. 2, n. 3).

20. Doc. Log No. 01-1546-69 (Confidential), dated February 10, 1969. Translation of a circular dated November 26, 1968, issued by

Subregion 3, concerning the measures local Viet Cong units should institute to counter the GVN's Phuong Hoang program. Captured by the 9th U.S. Infantry Division on January 4, 1969.

21. Doc. Log No. 10-1679-66 (see Chap. 2, n. 3).

22. Doc. Log No. 07-1770-67 (see Chap. 2, n. 3).

23. *Ibid.*

24. Doc. Log No. 09-1357-67 (see Chap. 4, n. 66).

25. Doc. Log No. 08-1894-67 (see Chap. 4, n. 84) and Doc. Log No. 08-1954-67 (see Chap. 4, n. 83).

26. Doc. Log No. 06-1532-68 (Confidential), summarized in MACJ2 Bulletin No. 13,207, dated June 10, 1968. Summary of a notebook with entries dated between June 29, 1966, and April 2, 1968, maintained by a cadre of the Duy Xuyen District Security Section, Quang Da Province. Captured by the Americal Division on April 10, 1968.

27. Doc. Log No. 06-2406-68 (Confidential), summarized in MACJ2 Bulletin No. 13,665, dated June 25, 1968. Summary of a letter dated February 8, 1968, concerning the fomenting of mass uprisings in the towns and cities, and written by an unidentified cadre in the Tri-Thien-Hue Military Region. Captured by the 1st U.S. Air Cavalry Division.

28. Doc. Log No. 05-1131-68 (see Chap. 4, n. 14).

29. William L. Stearman, "Communist Terror Tactics in Viet-Nam," July 1968, p. 7 (unpublished memorandum).

30. *Ibid.*

31. Doc. Log No. 05-2754-68 (see Chap. 5, n. 17).

32. *Ibid.*

33. Doc. Log No. 04-3227-67 (Confidential), dated October 4, 1967. Translation of a Top Secret "Communiqué" concerning "The Struggle Against the Constituent Assembly Elections of the Puppets and Americans," issued by the Saigon-Gia Dinh Region Current Affairs Committee. Captured by the 1st U.S. Infantry Division on April 24, 1967.

34. *Ibid.*

35. Doc. Log No. 04-2598-67 (Confidential), dated April 26, 1967. Translation of an "Order" dated March 18, 1967, issued in the name of the People's Liberation Front Committee for Quang Nam Province. Captured by the 3d USMC Division on April 7, 1967.

36. *Ibid.*

37. See *The Saigon Post*, August 31 and September 1, 1967.

38. Cited in *Vietnam Report VII: The Presidential Election,*

166

Embassy of the Republic of Vietnam, Washington, D.C., p. 14.

39. *The New York Times*, March 24, 1969, p. C3.

40. *Ibid*.

41. Examples of Security Service circulars and letters concerning the need to investigate closely various "reactionary" political parties in South Vietnam were found in Doc. Log No. 11-2045-68 (Confidential), summarized in MACJ2 Bulletin No. 18,189, dated November 27, 1968; Doc. Log No. 01-1806-69 (Confidential), summarized in MACJ2 Bulletin No. 19,636, dated January 14, 1969; Doc. Log No. 10-1979-68 (Confidential), summarized in MACJ2 Bulletin No. 17,390, dated October 20, 1968; Doc. Log No. 10-1984-68 (Confidential), summarized in MACJ2 Bulletin No. 17,394, dated October 20, 1968; and Doc. Log No. 10-1989-68 (Confidential), summarized in MACJ2 Bulletin No. 17,397, dated October 21, 1968.

42. Robert Shaplen, "Viet Nam: Crisis of Indecision," *Foreign Affairs*, October 1967, pp. 95-110. For a somewhat different view on the possibilities for local accommodation, see Samuel P. Huntington, "The Bases of Accommodation," *Foreign Affairs*, July 1968, pp. 642-656.

43. General W. C. Westmoreland, USA, "Report on Operations in South Vietnam, January 1964-1968" (see Chap. 2, n. 63), p. 83.

44. Doc. Log No. 10-1795-68 (Confidential), dated November 24, 1968. Translation of a directive entitled "Actively Strengthen, Consolidate, and Develop the Revolutionary Administration and Restore the People's Control in Hamlets and Villages," issued by Subregion 3 in August 1968. Captured by the 9th U.S. Infantry Division on October 1, 1968.

45. Doc. Log No. 07-1868-67 (Confidential), dated July 19, 1967 (emphasis added). Translation of a directive entitled "Guideline for the Requirements of the 1966-1967 Troop Proselytizing Task," issued by the Current Affairs Committee of COSVN on October 30, 1966. Captured by the 25th U.S. Infantry Division on June 25, 1967.

46. For example, Doc. Log No. 03-5068-69 (Confidential), summarized in MACJ2 Bulletin No. 15, dated March 6, 1969. Summary of a directive dated January 27, 1969, attributed to an agency of Subregion 2, outlining the requirements for political struggles and troop proselytizing activities in conjunction with military and diplomatic attacks. Captured by the 82d U.S. Airborne Division on February 14, 1969.

0,167

47. Doc. Log No. 09-1942-68 (Confidential), dated October 30, 1968. Extract translation of the 1968 "Directive—Pertaining to the Effort To Build A Revolutionary Administration at All Levels To Keep Pace with Developments of the Situation, in Execution of Directive # 13/CTNT [possibly COSVN]," attributed to the Current Affairs Committee of Subregion 3. Captured by the 9th U.S. Infantry Division on September 10, 1968.

48. Doc. Log No. 10-1795-68, emphasis added (see n. 44).

49. *Ibid.*

50. Doc. Log No. 01-3347-67 (see Chap. 2, n. 49).

51. Doc. Log No. 12-1877-67 (Confidential), summarized in MAC-J2 Bulletin No. 8454, dated December 14, 1967. Summary of a directive dated January 1, 1967, attributed to the Political Section of the Quang Nam Province Unit, which outlines security activities to be performed during 1967. Captured by the Americal Division on November 27, 1967. According to a Top Secret directive issued on July 27, 1967, by the Security Section of the Go Mon Subregion, a primary mission of all security cadres was to "study and discover the cadres' activities which are unfavorable for the observance of our mottos, our principles, and our policy of security maintenance." Doc. Log No. 01-1932-68 (Confidential), dated March 17, 1968. Captured by the 1st U.S. Infantry Division.

52. Viet Cong regulations specifically prohibit Communist cadres and other personnel from having any relations whatsoever with GVN personnel without official permission. For example, Doc. Log No. 04-2402-68 (Confidential), summarized in MACJ2 Bulletin No. 11,523, dated April 17, 1968. Captured by the 9th U.S. Infantry Division on April 9, 1968.

53. RM-5163/2-ISA/ARPA, *Origins of the Insurgency in South Vietnam, 1954-1960: The Role of the Southern Viet Minh Cadres*, by J. J. Zasloff, May 1968, p. 31.

54. *Ibid.*

55. The security measures envisaged by the Communists may be very stringent indeed. According to a Top Secret letter dated January 15, 1968, concerning the administrative measures to be taken after the "liberation" of Nha Be City, first priority was to be given to setting up the machinery to maintain law and order. Each city block of Nha Be was to have a security agent. In addition, one public security agent and two to three covert agents were to be planted among and control every fifty families. All "reactionary" individuals, "spies" and GVN public security

agents were to be searched out and arrested. Doc. Log No. 03-1983-63 (Confidential), summarized in MACJ2 Bulletin No. 10,437, dated March 18, 1968. Captured by the 9th U.S. Infantry Division on March 6, 1968.

56. An undated series of guidelines for political and military activities in My Tho Province stated that "after the establishment of local governments, the people's courts must be formed to eliminate the reactionaries (such as: returnees [defectors], spies, puppet administrative personnel and tyrants). Doc. Log No. 03-1970-68 (Confidential), dated March 27, 1968. Captured by the 9th U.S. Infantry Division on March 10, 1968.

57. Doc. Log No. 11-1020-68 (see Chap. 2, n. 24).

58. This was the policy followed during the Land Reform campaign in the North (Hoang Van Chi, *From Colonialism to Communism*, p. 95), and it is by no means alien to Communist practice in the South today. For example, a letter dated September 18, 1968, by the Political Staff of Subregion 4, intended to provide "Guidance on Propaganda Missions and [the] Motivation of the Masses During Combat in [the] Cities," stated that "we should: Rely on the Revolutionary people in local areas to detect and kill the puppet administrative personnel and tyrants." Doc. Log No. 03-5543-69 (Confidential), dated May 23, 1969. Captured by the 1st U.S. Infantry Division on March 20, 1969.

59. For the information on the concept of revenge in Vietnamese culture the author is indebted to his colleague Gerald C. Hickey.

Index

Selected Rand Books

Selected Rand Books

Becker, Abraham S. *Soviet National Income 1958-64*. Berkeley & Los Angeles: University of California Press, 1969.

Bergson, A. *The Real National Income of Soviet Russia Since 1928*. Cambridge, Mass.,: Harvard University Press, 1961.

Brodie, Bernard. *Strategy in the Missile Age*. Princeton, N.J.: Princeton University Press, 1959.

Davison, W. Phillips. *The Berlin Blockade: A Study in Cold War Politics*. Princeton, N.J.: Princeton University Press, 1958.

Dinerstein, H. S. *War and the Soviet Union: Nuclear Weapons and the Revolution in Soviet Military and Political Thinking*. New York: Frederick A. Praeger,1959.

Fainsod, Merle. *Smolensk Under Soviet Rule*. Cambridge Mass.: Harvard University Press, 1958.

Garthoff, Raymond L. *Soviet Military Doctrine*. Glencoe, Ill.: The Free Press, 1953.

George, Alexander L. *Propaganda Analysis: A Study of Inferences Made From Nazi Propaganda In World War II*. Evanston, Ill.: Row, Peterson and Company, 1959.

Gouré, Leon. *Civil Defense in the Soviet Union*. Los Angeles, Calif.: University of California Press, 1962.

Gouré, Leon. *The Siege of Leningrad*. Stanford, Calif.: Stanford University Press, 1962.

Gurtov, Melvin. *Southeast Asia Tomorrow: Problems and Prospects for US Policy*. Baltimore, Md.: The Johns Hopkins Press, 1970.

Halpern, Manfred. *The Politics of Social Change in the Middle East and North Africa*. Princeton, N.J.: Princeton University Press, 1963.

Hitch, Charles J., and Roland McKean. *The Economics of Defense in the Nuclear Age*. Cambridge, Mass.: Harvard University Press, 1960.

Horelick, Arnold L., and Myron Rush. *Strategic Power and Soviet Foreign Policy*. Chicago, Ill.: University of Chicago Press, 1966.

Hsieh, Alice Langley. *Communist China's Strategy in the Nuclear Era*. Englewood Cliffs, N.J.: Prentice-Hall, 1962.

Johnson, John J. (ed.). *The Role of the Military in Underdeveloped Countries*. Princeton, N.J.: Princeton University Press, 1962.

Kecskemeti, Paul. *The Unexpected Revolution*. Stanford, Calif.: Stanford University Press, 1961.

Kolkowicz, Roman. *The Soviet Military and the Communist Party*. Princeton, N.J.: Princeton University Press, 1967.

Kramish, Arnold. *Atomic Energy in the Soviet Union*. Stanford, Calif.: Stanford University Press, 1959.

Leites, Nathan. *A Study of Bolshevism*. Glencoe, Ill.: The Free Press, 1953.

Leites, Nathan. *The Operational Code of the Politburo*. New York: McGraw-Hill Book Company, 1951.

Leites, Nathan, and Charles Wolf, Jr. *Rebellion and Authority: An Analytic Essay on Insurgent Conflicts*. Chicago, Ill..: Markham Publishing Company, 1970.

Lubell, Harold. *Middle East Oil Crises and Western Europe's Energy Supplies*. Baltimore, Md.: The Johns Hopkins Press, 1963.

Pincus, John A. *Economic Aid and International Cost Sharing*. Baltimore, Md.: The Johns Hopkins Press, 1965.

Quade, E. S., and W. I. Boucher. *Systems Analysis and Policy Planning Applications in Defense*. New York: American Elsevier Publishing Co., 1968.

Rosen, George. *Democracy and Economic Change in India*. Berkeley and Los Angeles, Calif.: University of California Press, 1966.

Rush, Myron. *Political Succession in the USSR*. New York: Columbia University Press, 1965.

Rush, Myron. *The Rise of Khrushchev*. Washington, D.C.: Public Affairs Press, 1958.

Scalapino, Robert A. *The Japanese Communist Movement, 1920-1966*. Berkeley and Los Angeles, Calif.: University of California Press, 1967.

Sokolovskii, V. D. (ed.). *Soviet Military Strategy*. Englewood Cliffs, N.J.: Prentice-Hall, 1963.

Speier, Hans. *Divided Berlin: The Anatomy of Soviet Political Blackmail*. New York: Frederick A. Praeger, 1961.

Speier, Hans, and W. Phillips Davison (eds.). *West German Leadership and Foreign Policy*.Evanston, Ill.: Row, Peterson and Company, 1957.

Tanham, G. K. *Communist Revolutionary Warfare: The Vietminh in Indochina*. New York: Frederick A. Praeger, 1961.

Whiting, Allen S. *China Crosses the Yalu: The Decision to Enter the Korean War*. New York: The Macmillan Company, 1960.

Wolf, Charles, Jr. *Foreign Aid: Theory and Practice in Southern Asia*. Princeton, N.J.: Princeton University Press, 1960.

Wolfe, Thomas W. *Soviet Power and Europe 1945-1970*. Baltimore, Md.: The Johns Hopkins Press, 1970.

Wolfe, Thomas W. *Soviet Strategy at the Crossroads*. Cambridge, Mass.: Harvard University Press, 1964.